SOMEWHERE BEYOND

JESSIE KESSON (Jessie Grant McDonald) was born in October 1916 in Inverness. Her childhood was spent in Elgin with her mother—she never knew her father—until she was sent to the orphanage at Skene, Aberdeenshire. After leaving Skene school she entered service, and in 1934 moved to a farm with her husband, who was a cottar. She combined a successful writing career with a variety of jobs, from cleaner to artist's model, and was a social worker for nearly twenty years, settling finally in London with her husband.

The early years of her life influenced much of Jessie Kesson's writing. Her work includes the novels *The White Bird Passes* (1958), turned into an award-winning film in 1980, *Glitter of Mica* (1963), *Another Time, Another Place* (1983), which also became a prize-winning film, and the collection of short stories *Where the Apple Ripens* (1985). In addition, she wrote poetry, newspaper features, and plays for radio and television. Jessie Kesson died in 1994.

ISOBEL MURRAY is a Reader in English at the University of Aberdeen. Her publications include five annotated editions of the work of Oscar Wilde for Oxford University Press. Her Scottish work includes *Ten Modern Scottish Novels* (1984, with Bob Tait); two editions of the works of Naomi Mitchison, *Beyond This Limit* (1986) and *A Girl Must Live* (1990), and an Introduction to Mitchison's *Lobsters on the Agenda* (1997); a volume of interviews with Scottish writers which includes one with Jessie Kesson, *Scottish Writers Talking* (1996). She has written the biography of Jessie Kesson.

She is an Associate Editor of the *New Dictionary of National Biography*, with responsibility for Scottish writers since 1870; Vice-President of the Association of Scottish Literary Studies; and a member of the panel which selects the Saltire Book of the Year.

OTHER B&W TITLES BY JESSIE KESSON

THE WHITE BIRD PASSES

ANOTHER TIME, ANOTHER PLACE

GLITTER OF MICA

WHERE THE APPLE RIPENS

JESSIE KESSON

SOMEWHERE BEYOND

EDITED AND INTRODUCED BY
ISOBEL MURRAY

B&W PUBLISHING

This volume first published 2000
by B&W Publishing Ltd
Edinburgh

ISBN 1 903265 01 0

The publisher acknowledges subsidy
from the Scottish Arts Council towards
the publication of this volume.

British Library Cataloguing in Publication Data:
A catalogue record for this book is available
from the British Library

Cover design by *Winfortune & Co*

Cover illustration:
Detail from *Rest Time in the Life Class* (1923)
by Dorothy Johnstone ARSA (1892–1980)
Reproduced by courtesy of
City of Edinburgh Museums and Art Galleries
Photograph: The Bridgeman Art Library

Printed by WS Bookwell

CONTENTS

INTRODUCTION

Isobel Murray

'Bring I to my days an eager joy'

Jessie Kesson was born illegitimate in disgrace and penury at the Workhouse in Inverness in 1916, and lived her first ten years in Elgin with her unpredictable mother. Her mother combined poverty, small-time prostitution and a weakness for drink with a great love of the countryside, and a vast knowledge of poetry. These loves she shared with her daughter, who learned reams of nineteenth-century poetry on long barefoot country walks, in a most unusual version of what is known as the oral tradition.

Aged ten, Kesson was legally removed from her mother on grounds of neglect, and sent to an Orphanage in Skene, Aberdeenshire. This was the first and indeed the best of many institutions she was to pass through, each time leaving a familiar milieu and facing alone an unknown community and having to adapt to it. Proctor's Orphan Training Home was small, housing up to eight children at a time, and if the regime was not loving, neither was it unkind or over-strict. She went on to excel at Skene School, where the head teacher, her beloved 'dominie', encouraged her to aim for Higher Education at the University of Aberdeen. As she vividly records in her first novel, *The White Bird Passes*, the orphanage Trustees firmly denied this ambition, which would have been seen as over-inflated even for a male orphan at the 'Training Home', which generally prepared children for domestic or farm service. So she was denied Higher Education. Her regrets stayed with her, as we can see in the poem 'A Scarlet Goon', written when she was twenty-nine, and had become a 'cottar wife' on a series of north-east farms. After a series of disastrous attempts to conform to conventional expectations about her future, she spent a year in the mental hospital in Aberdeen. Released 'on probation' and boarded-out at Abriachan, a tiny village high above Inverness, she met and married John Kesson in 1937. They were farm-workers in north-east Scotland for a number of years, with Kesson writing first for periodicals and then for the BBC in Scotland. Much of this writing attempted to come to terms with the extraordinary and often sanity-threatening circumstances of her youth.

In 1951, they set out for London with their daughter and son to further Jessie's literary and broadcasting ambitions. For the next four decades Jessie combined running a home, endlessly writing, and working in hard physical jobs, often in institutions. She published four volumes of fiction at understandably long intervals; *The White Bird Passes* in 1958, *Glitter of Mica* in 1963, *Another Time, Another Place* in 1983, and *Where the Apple Ripens and Other Stories* in 1985. She continued to write for radio, and was described by Stewart Conn as 'one of the finest of for-radio writers'. She achieved national recognition in 1980, when Michael Radford's prize-winning television adaptation of *The White Bird Passes* was universally applauded, and she wrote the novel *Another Time, Another Place*, published in 1983, while she and Radford collaborated to create the film. The film won fourteen international awards.

A wealth of Kesson's writing, especially for radio, did not see the light of print. Jessie and her husband both died in 1994, at which time she had still not produced her long-promised autobiography, *Mistress of None.*

'My heart has a vivid colour, I know'

She found the matter of the autobiography impossibly difficult. In one sense this is strange, because so much of her writing was at least in part autobiographical. She changed the projected title, after Thoreau, to *A Different Drum*, reinforcing her sense of being an outsider wherever she went, an 'ootlin' as she called it, marching to a different beat from other people. At one stage she projected an autobiographical account of the London years, *When I Set Out for Lyonesse*, but that too remained an unrealised dream. While a great deal of her work was to some extent or another autobiographical, finding a mode, a tone, a form that would encompass the intensely-varied whole seemed impossible.

Kesson should have been crushed or emotionally destroyed by the horrors of her childhood, and the series of partings that littered it, starting with the painful break with her mother. She should surely have had her spirit crushed by the series of institutions—orphanage, hostel for girls on probation, mental hospital. She refused to be crushed. But there is a sense in which she was possessed and oppressed by her childhood almost all her life. When she left the mental hospital, she was offered no after-care, no care of any kind. So what she did was to act as her own psychotherapist. One way to look at her writing is to see it almost as a series of exorcisms. She had to express both the pain and the excitement and happiness of a lost past, lost in part because she had no one to share the past with. Time and again she wrote about the Elgin slum that was her first remembered home, about the grandmother she adored and the grandfather who refused to acknowledge her existence. She looked for a unity in her life, in her self, a reassurance that she was a coherent character, a person with some kind of continuity. And in the course of her 'self-therapy' she produced enchanting works which have had an enormous impact on readers.

This volume aims to let readers see the unknown or forgotten Kesson, the artist at work. It demonstrates the working out of some central themes by offering examples of her writing over fifty years. It opens with 'Railway Journey', the very first surviving example where the artist tried to write out the paradoxical childhood, unorthodox mother as against ultra-orthodox matron, Elgin as against Skene, slum as against orphanage. Kesson was not to be fully satisfied with a treatment of this area until she published *The White Bird Passes* in 1958. On one hand, it is astonishing that so much of the future novel is already here in embryo, in this short two-part piece: on the other, it is very informative to notice what is later removed. The miracle of *The White Bird Passes* lies partly in the expression of the child's vivid love for and delight in both slum and orphanage. That is what remains in the mind, rather than pain or resentment. But in 'Railway Journey' there is a note of bitterness. Kesson knew her mother would not see the piece, or be hurt by it, and anonymous publishing in a small magazine was not going to expose either mother or daughter to the kind of tabloid headline one paper later found for *The White Bird*:

Mother's secrets told:
DAUGHTER SHOWS NO SHAME.

So here she can describe Liz as 'the mother who loved me in her own bitter way', and the slum population as 'poor and hungry and bitter'. And the poem that consoles her picks up that note again: 'Love much, Life has enough of bitterness in it'. Clearly Kesson taught herself kinds of concealment or pruning, dependent on circumstances. It was Ruskin who described his autobiography as 'the natural me . . . only peeled carefully'. A letter to publisher Peter Calvocoressi shows her awareness of the possibilities of causing hurt. She was notifying him that the second 'Childhood' play, her own story, was to be repeated yet again and hoping he would manage to listen:

> I do hope you will hear the broadcast on Tuesday. It was written long ago, when Dominie, Matron, Trustees were still alive; as was my mother. So that I have not altered one word of it, to tie up with *White*

Bird. My mother being alive then, I could not bear to portray her as fully as in *White Bird.* And the others also being alive, I had no need to devise either hopeful or happy endings, but the true ending.

'Railway Journey' balances the two lives that pull the girl in such different directions. In 1990 Colette Douglas-Home presented this account of an interview in *The Scotsman*:

> Day after day she climbed a local hill. 'If I looked down on one side I could see buses going to Elgin where my mother was. If I looked down on the other side I could see the orphanage and the farm. I was torn between wondering where I should go and I took a nervous breakdown'.

Here the journey itself is an effective means of dramatising her quandary. Where will the girl find a home? And already we sense that she will have no continuing city until she builds one for herself, with words. The protagonist of this story has to go back physically in order to learn that she cannot recapture the past. As we learn from 'Somewhere Beyond', Kesson used to run away from the Aberdeen hostel with its vindictive matron, to try to get back physically to the orphanage, and beyond that to the Lane. But she early learned the futility of such attempts to recapture time past. Her work echoes her awareness repeatedly, from the story about Abriachan in *Where the Apple Ripens*, called 'Road of No Return', to the radio talk here, 'We Can't Go Back'. It was on paper or on air that almost all the meaningful return journeys would be made.

But one symbolic journey *was* made, which meant more to Kesson than even its instigator could have foreseen. In 1987 Sir Kenneth Alexander was appointed Chancellor to the University of Aberdeen, and was invited to propose four recipients of Honorary Degrees to mark his installation. He nominated Jessie Kesson. In 1985 when I interviewed the writer in depth on tape, I found she still resented the mean-spirited orphanage Trustees who had refused her the chance to go to Aberdeen University, to undertake the Higher Education she so much desired. She firmly resisted my well-meant platitudes about what she had made of her life, and insisted,

> but my life would have been on different lines . . . it was something I should have had, I would have loved every—Oh, I canna explain, not even to you, I know my life would have been awfa' different'. (*Scottish Writers Talking*, p 74.)

Sir Kenneth's gift did more to salve that resentment than he could have imagined. The graduation was a most moving experience. And it was closely associated with another. Most of Kesson's school classmates still lived in Skene, or Aberdeenshire more generally, and to celebrate the degree they held a reunion lunch in her honour. This was as near as her dislocated life could get to a triumphant return home. The television play 'The Reunion', almost the last thing Kesson wrote, shows the force of the symbolic occasion, and in a sense at last completes the return journey.

'I think even mair than the book, I like radio better, because of the sound of the words'.

This volume shows very clearly that Kesson's work is not a series of cries of pain—quite the reverse. The best single adjective seems to me to be 'celebratory'. Kesson loved her mother, and the Lane in Elgin: she loved the orphanage at Skene, and the dominie who taught her there. She made the most of every environment she was thrust into. After her mother, most of all she loved words, like Danny Kernon in 'The Childhood':

I belonged so fully to my own mind, to the brave words I learned in school, to the things my eyes saw, to the music my ears heard.

Every reader of her work will have been struck by the stream of music that runs through her work. Kesson heard poetry long before she read it, and its sound was very important to her. Her books are full of the tunes that run in her protagonists' heads—the traditional songs Janie learned from 'the Mannie' at the orphanage, the stream of hymns and popular songs, mission choruses and children's games that flows with her, as with Isabel in 'Where the Apple Ripens', the way Helen Mavor used to recite poetry in the class above; the excitement of Paddy the piper in 'Anybody's Alley'. Danny Kernon, the protagonist of 'The Childhood', was inspired by the paraphrase he sang in church to run on the hill 'like a mad thing', and it was singing 'The Meeting of the Waters' at school that opened his eyes to the wonder of Loch Ness:

'I'd gone so often before, but I never really saw it till the day we learned to sing 'The Meeting of the Waters' at school'.

In a very wide sense, then, in spite of her medical history, Kesson was 'of sound mind'. This makes it particularly ironic that so much of her delight in words has been hidden from us by the failure to publish or otherwise make available to us any of her radio work. This volume begins to open up the field. Kesson wrote and herself read 'A Scarlet Goon' on radio in 1945. She read 'Saturday Night' on the Third Programme in 1960. 'We Can't Go Back' was a talk for *Woman's Hour* in 1957, and she spent a very happy and fulfilled year working full time for that programme in 1961. And included here are three centrally important plays, 'The Childhood', 'Somewhere Beyond' and 'Reunion'. I have touched on 'Reunion' already. 'The Childhood' is a particularly good example of the transient nature of radio production, although in this case some blame must attach to Kesson herself. It was she who wrote the play in 1949 as 'The Childhood'—and then followed it in 1952 with a completely different play also entitled 'The Childhood'! The second play was immensely successful, and often repeated: it was a radio version of the material to be treated in *The White Bird Passes*. But it effectively obscured the previous success of this play, which led to the nearest Kesson ever came to what we could call political action. It is a unique blend of imagination and autobiographical feeling. Its protagonist is a ten-year-old Glasgow boy who has been removed from a mother with a drink problem and 'boarded-out' in the hamlet of Abriachan, high above Loch Ness.

Kesson felt strongly about the plight of some boarded-out children, who were removed from the surroundings they knew as well as from their families. When the Kesson family was living at Linksfield she had habitually and quietly helped the Elgin Welfare Officer with these children's problems behind the scenes. They were often city children, despatched to sparsely populated areas with ageing populations. Her own husband, John Kesson, and his siblings had been boarded out at Abriachan in childhood, but they were lucky enough to have had a good and kindly foster mother, who did all she could to make them happy. Not all boarded-out children were similarly lucky: many were exploited and overworked, even ill-treated, and received no affection or care. Kesson herself experienced boarding out at age nineteen, when she was sent to Abriachan direct from the mental hospital in Aberdeen, to live with a very old woman who needed her help on the croft. She was known as 'The Patient', and young men were warned not to talk to her. Out of all this Kesson produced a play that caused a considerable furore and much public discussion: this was a hot public issue. The play was repeated many times. In 1950 Kesson was asked to give evidence to a Scottish Home Department committee investigating boarding out, as someone who could speak for the recipients or victims, who had never been consulted in any previous exercise. She gave it, and her advice was heeded.

'Somewhere Beyond' needed to be written. Kesson had avoided as much as possible writing about her post-

Skene experiences. She *had* achieved a fine account of her mental hospital experience in the radio play 'And That Unrest'. But she needed to write a fuller account, one that connected the horrors of mental hospital with the events which had led up to it for the disoriented teenager, giving coherence to perhaps the hardest part of her life. She understood that need: in spite of the endorsements given to the radio play, she wrote to Peter Calvocoressi:

> Was pleasantly surprised to find repeat of 'Somewhere Beyond' referred to in this week's *Listener*, since it was well reviewed there by a different critic on its first transmission. It *is* one of the things I *would* like to write in permanent form. What do you think? I mean, would C&W be interested?

But once it had been produced on radio, and well-received, Kesson was able to move on to other things: we find her latterly dissatisfied with the audience's obsession with her early childhood, and writing about a number of new issues, like the problems of teenage girls in institutions, in 'You Never slept in Mine!', or the painful realities of growing old, in 'Dear Edith . . .' and 'Three Score and Ten, Sir!', actually set in London, the latter especially showing her hard-gained mastery of Cockney intonation.

Effectively, the physician had healed herself.

DEDICATION

In our interview with Jessie Kesson, printed in *Scottish Writers Talking* (1996), Jessie said:

> I love radio and I'll tell you why. Because words mean so much to radio and words and the sound and the meaning of them is *my* thing. I love radio. And I've aye been very, very lucky in my producers; they did it very, very brilliantly you know.

This volume is dedicated to all those who worked with Jessie on radio over many decades, and especially to these:

Elizabeth Adair
Moultrie R Kelsall
James Crampsey
Archie P Lee
Joanna Scott-Moncrieff
Dorothy Baker
David Thomson
Stewart Conn
Gordon Emslie
James Hunter
Marilyn Imrie

PART I

EARLY STORIES

RAILWAY JOURNEY

I

THE girl in the corner of the railway carriage wasn't finding the going-back journey pleasant. It recalled too vividly the going-away journey nine years earlier.

. . . Kind 'Cruelty' man! 'Don't cry for your mother,' you said, patting my head, 'you're going to a nice orphanage, where you'll be well cared for, and get plenty to eat.'

I didn't want to go to a nice orphanage. I didn't want plenty to eat. I just wanted to jump out of the carriage and run home to my mother. But he didn't understand. I was too young to bear malice; and blows get better. It was only the ache inside me that was never going to get better.

I wasn't crying for the Liz McLean you know. I was crying for the mother who loved me in her own bitter way; I was crying for the good companion who could tell wonderful stories, for the woman who 'loved all beauteous things'. This I never told him; he might have laughed; and I had a deep dread of ridicule. But he wouldn't have understood . . . Kind 'Cruelty' man . . .

Goodbye Kelbie's Close. I was nine when I left it, but

I'd never been young. I learned the facts of life crudely with the alphabet. Kelbie's Close saw to that.

Life was: eating when there was food; fighting when there was drink; and . . . 'all along a dirtiness, all along a mess, all along a finding out rather more than less'.

When I left school I was heart-broken, but I hated it when I was in Kelbie's Close. I sat alone, removed from respectable children. The teacher ignored me as much as possible. Dress and address were of more importance to her than a dirty little girl's feelings. Teaching was her job, not her vocation. She didn't see beneath the dirt.

Finding the real world a sordid place, I escaped to a secret world. 'Hiawatha' was the first poem to make a lasting impression on me; and the stories of Ancient Greece got so deeply into my imagination that:

I wad ha'e made a wudden' horse
  Oot o' ilka aiken tree,
An' cut the rowans intae spears
  For the sake o' chivalry.

And so I was never lonely in my imaginary world of Indian Braves and Greek Heroes. When school was dismissed I left that world behind and ran back to Kelbie's Close . . . to run amok . . . Down to the caravan encampments which always fascinated me. Sitting round the fires, unkempt, but always vital, terribly interested in these uncouth, wandering folk, who like myself were just so much flotsam and jetsam . . . We had no roots . . . This was affinity.

'The 'Cruelty' man's doon at the camps,' someone would remark. Off I would run, filled with a pleasant fear at the nearness of danger, safe in the knowledge of the back-wynds.

All things end. I was taken, unexpectedly, to a courtroom, and questioned endlessly. I saw my mother so terribly alone, and something fiercely protective rose up inside me. 'Never mind them!' I wanted to cry to her. 'I love you, I know you're good.' I knew blindly that sometime something had gone wrong with her. Life being ruthless . . .

But these smug men sat condemning! It's so easy to condemn. What right had they to judge Kelbie's Close from the sheltered security of their suburban villas? They knew of it from their police records; but they didn't live there, where people were poor and hungry and bitter. But for the Grace of God and the force of circumstances every one of them stood in the dock.

I shall never forget my first impression of the Orphanage. I thought then, and still do, that it was the loveliest place I had ever seen. There was nothing of the institution about it. In structure it was like an old English mansion and it was approached by a long tree-lined avenue. In front of the house was a large lawn bordered with lilies. I never saw so many lilies! And I can never think of the Orphanage without thinking of lilies. Above the front door was the inscription: Proctor's Kirkville Orphan Training Home 1891. I remember it well because I was marched round to read it every time I forgot to dust beneath the beds.

The inside proved as much of a joy. A big range glowed, big windows shone, and the woodwork was spotlessly white. Everything about the Orphanage was big and shining.

'Do you think you'll like to stay with us?' the matron—a middle-aged, homely woman—asked me. I parried her question. 'Will I get home when I'm fourteen?' I asked.

I went to the district school next day. I wasn't too happy. You see, on arrival at the Orphanage my hair was cut off and to cover this deficiency I wore a large straw hat of many colours. I was conscious that I looked odd in my heavy boots and summer hat, but nothing could persuade me to take my hat off in school. It was my helmet against ridicule.

I had to sit in the bottom seat till I got my place in class, much to the discomfort of the seat's other occupant, Charlie Anderson, who disconcerted me by asking the others 'If that was a loon or a quean?' I told him quite firmly I was a 'quean', but he wasn't to be convinced. I was second in the test and when I went to my seat the others laughed. 'That girl will surprise you one day,' the teacher said. Perhaps she said it to take the edge off their laughter . . . But I never quite forgave Charlie for not discerning the eternal woman.

II

'The days that make us happy make us wise'. I soon adjusted myself to the new life I had to lead in the Orphanage. Fear became a thing of the past, and because

I was tidy and clean, I began to feel like other children. But there was always this restless undercurrent, always this sensitiveness to life. I never quite lost it.

Mrs Ellis was kept too busy feeding and cleaning us to have much time to love us, but she was very kind and very just. Twice a year she took us all into Aberdeen—at Christmas and in the summer holidays. These two days were the highlights of the year. We looked forward to them weeks ahead. The first time I was taken to Aberdeen I was so excited that I got ready at ten o'clock the night before. I put on all my finery and made a round of the dormitories, illustrating what we would do on the beach, much to the delight of the other excited children. Then, feeling very exuberant, I slid down the bannisters and collided with Mrs Ellis who, hearing the hilarity, was waiting for me at the bottom of the stairs. She didn't punish me, but said that it would be wiser to leave me at home as the excitement wouldn't be good for me. I nearly had a nightmare. Next morning, however, Mrs Ellis repented of her decision and I was taken along with the others. But my escape was so narrow that I never again gave a preview before the big event.

Books were plentiful at the Orphanage. I read avidly anything and everything. My taste was catholic.

Poetry was my greatest love. The deep joy of discovering, in my journeys through the realms of gold, some new poems other than the poems we had to learn by heart—poems which one guarded in one's heart, jealous lest someone else should discover their beauty.

Love much, Life has enough of bitterness in it,
Cast sweets into its cup whene'er you can,
No heart so hard but love at last may win it,
Love is the grand, primeval quest of man.
All hate is foreign to the first great plan.
Love much, men's hearts contract with cold suspicion.
Shine on them with warm love and they expand,
It's love alone that from a low condition
Leads mankind up to heights sublime and grand,
Oh, that the world could see and understand.

I began writing poetry; and English being my strong point at school the good dominie encouraged me. 'You've got the gift,' he said. 'I hope you develop it, but hurry slowly.'

Only now and then the old Ness of Kelbie's Close would emerge to wreck the calm of my days. I would feel a restless longing for the caravans, for the hilarity of Saturday nights, for the old, wild freedom. Something would go wrong at the Orphanage, and in the best language of Kelbie's Close I would let them know about it. Mrs Ellis and the children looked askance at me, and I would feel ashamed. Nobody spoke to me for a day or two. Naturally warm and impulsive, I felt this far worse than a thrashing. I froze up inside, and went about with a cold, shut-out feeling. I prayed very hard: 'Dear God, make Mrs Ellis and the kids be friends with me again, and I won't swear again.' When I was taken back into the fold, I was sure that God did it.

After I had taken the Day School Higher Certificate—

this was as far as the Higher Grade School went—the dominie started to coach me for the prelims. He gave me all the books necessary, and said he would pay the entrance fee himself. But this didn't come off.

When I was sixteen I was sent to work at a farm in the district. In between scrubbing floors and feeding hens, I still pursued poetry and, with the sublime confidence of the young, thought often and often:

I'll follow my secret heart,
my whole life through,
I'll keep all my dreams apart,
Till one comes true.

The train was nearing its destination and the girl in the corner seat began to show signs of life.

I'll soon know which is the real me—Ness of the Orphanage, or Ness of Kelbie's Close. Has everything changed, or is the change just in myself? I haven't forgotten; it's all too vivid. The years don't bring forgetfulness. 'Surely ye min' on Ness McLean—Liz McLean's dochter. They used tae bide in Kelbie's Close. A'body kent them.' Of course, that's what they'll say. I should have, I must have known it all along. I'll never escape Ness of Kelbie's Close.

Can you tell me when the next train leaves for Aberdeen? And may I have a single ticket. I should have taken a return, you know, but I'm very stupid.

FERM DEEM

ROSE bided in their minds lang efter a succession o' Maggies, Bells and Jeans war juist annoyin' memories. Makin' a bed was ae thing Rose could dae really weel—next till her aptitude for sleepin' in ane. Alarum clocks did nothing tae Rose, nor did Dykie himsel', kickin' at her closet door wi' his muckle tacketty beets, disturb the slumbers o' Rose. Naething short o' the mistress hersel' comin' a' the wye doon the stairs and through the steen lobby in her bare feet, a blue goon wallopin' roon' her, an' her hair hingin' owre her face like an Amazon gaun in ti battle, had ony effect on Rose, wha wasna immune tae the blankets bein' thrown off her and the mistress's scornful epithets dingin' in her lugs.

'Ye muckle lazy hulk, lyin' there steamin', fan the men wull be in in twa-three meenits for their porridge. It's nae muckle langer I'll pit up wi' your didos!'

Rose wad open her een tae view the mornin' wraths wi' a placidity that drove Dykie's mistress intae fair fury—and, as the day wore on, melted it doon tae contempt.

'She's nae a' there, of coorse!' the mistress wad confide

tae the cattlie and the horseman owre their breakfast, fan Rose was weel oot o' hearin' un'er the coos' teuch udders in the byre.

Syne, fan Rose cam' in and the men war oot o' hearin', the mistress wad confide tae Rose.

'What a belly that cattlie his! Fower quarters o' breid stappit intil't afore ye could see them disappearin'.'

That was the mistress's wye; fowk's little failin's gied her a hantle pleasure, though she wis aye careful tae describe thae failin's ahint their backs—a' except Rose's back. Rose ranked low doon in even the mistress's low estimate o' fowk. There was naebody tae worry aboot fat was said tae Rose, and Rose didna care muckle hersel'.

Rose's first memories war o' the impersonal poor-hoose; syne the boarded-oot days at Couther's Hill faur there wis ither twa boarded-oot bairns, a coo, a croft, an' jist the mistress tae work it wi' the help o' the bairns. That left the mistress wi' jist time tae be gweed tae the bairns, but nae enough time tae be kind tae them. Rose was weel fed, weel claithed, her closet up the stair was clean, her bed smelt fresh, like the byres at nicht fan they war newly strawed. Bit, though the mistress nivir saw Rose an' the ither twa bairns hungry for mate, she wis jist aye owre hashed tae speir fit wye they war greetin', unless there wis ony sign o' bleed comin' fae a sair.

Even in bairnhood, Rose nivir found time tae be blithe. School was agony. Rose could coont wi' her fingers, bit, fan she wis nearly fourteen itsel', she couldna read muckle further than the first class's book. She could nivir write; she jist sat and loot the clivir bairns cry her: 'Duncie squint-een! Duncie squint-een!' and hoped the time wad sune flee in so that she could win hame and spend the rest o' the nicht pu'in' neeps for the coo, carryin' strae tae the byre, and gaun tae the well for water.

Life was jist daein' things forivir for some superior, first for the poor-hoose matron, syne for Couther Hill's mistress; ahint that, fan Rose gaed tae her first place, for Mrs Danny. That was the only time that Rose ivir felt she was Rose; somebody that was actually a bein', and her name was Rose.

Mrs Danny was instrumental in the rehabilitation of Rose. Mrs Danny, stoot, slow, abune the demands o' the cuckoo-clock in the sitting room; that wag-at-the-wa' in the kitchen; the alarum clock in the bedroom; made time for hersel' tae contemplate the sma' squint-e'ed craittur that skookit like a fast futrett in the domains o' the scullery, kitchen, byre, hen-hooses—and jist on a Friday—the bedrooms an' ben-the-hoose.

Rose's response tae ony personal interest in hersel' was slow, but it took haud. A warmth tingled a' owre her skin the day Mrs Danny airmed, warrior-like, wi' a sheers, clippit a bit aff o' Rose's lank, colourless hair—nae as the poor-hoose matron did, or Couther's Hill's mistress either, wi' the intention 'o' haudin't frae straggling in o' yer een',—bit, as Mrs Danny said, 'tae mak ye bonny'.

Rose was conscious eneuch o' ither quines' bonniness, bit the fact that she'd nae claims tae beauty didna bother her. Tae get her sleep, her diet, her work daen atween risin'-time and beddin'-time was Rose's reason for livin'.

She nivir took her day aff aince a fortnicht; there wis nae wye tae tak' a day aff till, and naebody tae share it wi'. She felt ony spare time lie heavy on her han's; she nivir acquired the gift o' usin' time for her ain pleasure.

Mrs Danny hadna stoppit the gweed work at the clippin' o' the hair. Rose had twenty paper pounds anent her six months' work. Mrs Danny took her a' the wye tae MacIlwraith's Stores and turned eicht o' the pounds intae first, 'For yer byre, an' gaun owre the parks tae feed yer hens in the winter, a pair o' stoot sheen; twa pairs o' thick stockin's, warm underclaes, twa dark workin' overalls; twa licht-floo'ered overalls for afterneen, a broon coat wi' a bit fur at its neck for best, and a green frock wi' a collar that wad come off for washin' tae gang onywys special in!'

O' the twelve pounds that remained tae tell o' Rose's six months' wark, six Mrs Danny had keepit in her ain drawer in the bedroom, 'for,' she explained tae Rose, 'tae haud ye gaun through the neist six months.' The ither six pounds was written doon in a green savings-book, wi' the name Rose Irvine written on't, and it wis keepit, efter mony admonishments fae Mrs Danny, tae 'be careful wi't, an' keep addin' till't'—in the bottom o' Rose's ain kist.

That day spent wi' Mrs Danny penetrated even Rose's mind. It was something greater than manners that urged 'thank ye' in the form o' Rose sayin' till Mrs Danny: 'You pey yer ain tea as well as mine oot o' my six pounds that's nae bankit.' And it wasna meanness that gaured Mrs Danny accept her paid tea quickly and definitely.

Bit that wis far awa' noo, nearly lost oot o' mind. Efter that, Rose's real troubles began.

Mair than Mrs Danny took it intae their heids that Rose wis a human as weel as a servant. Dod, the orra-lad, divined it, and though Mrs Danny's humanity brocht gratitude tae life in Rose, Dod's airms roond her amang the strae brocht warmth tae life.

Mrs Danny wis a lot mair anger't wi' Dod than ivir she was wi' Rose, and tell't him so wi' barbit tongue. 'Takin' advantage o' a simple craittur like her, wi' nae thocht o' marryin', either. Nae that it wad be a gweed thocht. A pair o' simpletons nivir made a wise thing yet.'

So, fan Rose found it owre muckle an effort tae sit un'er the coos, an' was owre heavy an' dizzy tae thole bakin' the breid on the hot range, Mrs Danny added ither twenty pounds tae the six in the green bank-book, sayin': 'Ye'll need them a', lassie. A body peys dear for stolen comfort.' And Rose was back faur she began in Kirktowie poor-hoose.

Gratitude slippit awa' fae Rose wi' fleeter feet than it cam' tae her. Dykie's mistress was the type Rose had aye kent. Mrs Danny turned intil an unreal memory oot o' an unreal time. The new mistress hadna even the spark o' kindness at term-time peyin' Rose. Instead, she'd the glint o' hardness. She'd a lang sheet o' paper as weel, and doon on't wi' mair accuracy than God Himsel' wad use in writin' Judgement Book, she'd written: 'Broken by Rose Irvine.'

Rose, nae bein' a reader hersel', listened tae the date o' breakin', and the articles broken, wi' a feelin' that she'd done naething else ilka day for six months bit let fa'!

One saucer from Willow Pattern service........ 8d
Men's brown teapot.................................. 2s.9d
Broke new clothes rope............................. 5s.6d

Two tumblers	1s.6d
Fell with basket, broke 17 eggs	3s.9d

And so Dykie's mistress handed her a lot less than Mrs Danny wi' a lot less gweedwill. Jist as the better Rose cam' tae life wi' Mrs Danny, so did the waur Rose hae bein' wi' Dykie's mistress. Afore, Rose had taen owregauns as a maitter o' fact. Flytin' was something she was used till. She'd lang since learned nae only tae tak' it a' in silence, but tae put it clean oot o' her mind till neist time. But since she'd laen in the strae wi' the warmth o' Dod beside her, and for a' that the poor-hoose wi' its unspoken hostility had been the ootcome o't, Rose had discovered there was mair tae livin' than jist flytin' and workin', and this mair was warm and better and pleased Rose abune a'thing she'd ivir kent.

Rose felt her dislike for Dykie's mistress intensify ilka time the men cam' intae the kitchen; for syne Dykie's mistress's tongue excelled itsel'; it was as if an audience consistin' o' the cattlie and horsemen gied her an incentive, a finer thing than jist layin' forth till a queer, white-faced quine fa nivir showed resentment itsel', bit jist dadded on as though she, Dykie's mistress, was jist speakin' till hersel'.

Rose's predecessors, Maggies, Bellas and Jeans, had at least gien her the pleasure o' a gweed bicker back and fore, bit there wis nae winnin' tae the bottom o' this Rose quine at a'. Of coorse, she was jist simple, bit for a' that, Dykie's mistress felt that the besom, simple or no', aye got the better o' her wi' jist keepin' a calm sough.

It wasna easy for Rose tae keep quate, nae efter Dod

had been sae lovin' and kind, and had gien Rose the feelin' that if there couldna aye be Dod, there could be some ither kind, lovin' ane, and he micht come in the shape o' the cattlie or Bill, the horseman—but they'd nivir come, nae wi' that ill-tongued wife aye stanin' sayin' things that gaur'd even Rose burn up inside hersel'.

'Isna she jist a clart? Look at Bill's speen! He winna sup soup wi' bits o' porridge aye stickin' till the speen. An' ye micht tak' off that big bag apron ye've been scrubbin' wi', an' gie the men their mate clean like.'

Dimly intae Rose's mind cam' the thochts that harpin' on aboot sticky speens, and aprons an' clarts wad feenish ony thocht o' lovin' in the strae in ony chield's mind, and Rose couldna gie her thochts words an cry oot:

'I hinna time! I hinna a meenit fae the time I rise till the time I lie doon. It's jist a rush tae get things dune, whether they're richt dune or no, wi' bairns clamourin' roon' ma feet in the middle o' a'thing, greetin' for this an' that, an' haen tae stop and see till them or she'll raise auld Harry, an' she aye stan's harpin' on an' on, instead o' gien's a han'. I nivir ken faur I've began, nor faur I've stoppit.'

The festerin' thochts that Rose couldna put intae words grew intae a hateful sair idea. Ilka warpit day brocht the idea tae a heid, the idea had nae richt shape nor form, it wis jist an idea tae hurt back in some wye that wad hurt this coorse-tonged Dykie's mistress.

The cattlie brocht it tae a heid, comin' in as he aye did at ten in the mornin' for het water for the kye's drink. The dance brocht it till a heid, tae, nae that Rose had ony thocht o' the dance; she couldna dance a step, an' she tellt the cattlie that. 'Nivir mind aboot dancin'; jist ask till't,' he advised. 'Ye dinna need tae dance, and I'll see ye hame'.

Of coorse it was naething mair than Rose expected fae Dykie's mistress—a refusal—but what a refusal!

'Dance! Ye canna rise oot o' yer bed, nivir heed dance! An' the cattlie askit ye, did he? He wis jist pullin' yer leg. The cattlie's got mair pride in himsel' than trail you till a dance.'

'Ye'll need tae see that she washes her neck richt afore ye tak' her dancin', an' if she gangs there a trollop like fit she gangs here, ye'll get a red neck yersel'.'

And the cattlie had jist turned red, and lauched, and said in a sheepish wye: 'Och, I was jist teasin' her aboot the dance.'

What a moment that was for Dykie's mistress! An' what triumph was in her voice! 'I kent the cattlie had mair sense. He wis jist pu'in' yer leg.'

Rose wasna that thick bit fat she kent the cattlie had jist wriggled oot o' the dance; he'd aince intendit takin' her. It wis Dykie's mistress wi' her tongue that pit him aff.

She wadna hae been a trollop either; nae wi' the green frock wi' the collar, that Mrs Danny had bocht for her. She'd jist aince worn it—nae here, though—she'd nivir haen time, an' the cattlie had nivir seen her in that frock, and nae likely he'd see her in't now.

She felt stiff and cauld inside wi' dislike for Dykie's mistress; she'd nivir felt like that afore. She washed the supper-plates withoot seein' them; her e'en were glued tae the scullery-window seein' naething there either. There was naething tae see except the great rucks o' corn;

gradually thocht began tae function again through the cauldness; the rucks set it gaun. They war to be threshed the morn; she'd baked owre the hot range a' efterneen for the threshin'-mill the morn; what a day o't she'd hae the morn; she'd be fair run aff her feet. Dykie's mistress wad be a' dressed up, lauchin' tae the mannies an' handin' roon the platres o' scones jist as though she'd steed owre the fire an' bake't them a'. That was like Dykie's mistress. Eh, hoo Rose hated her. The idea took form withoot Rose thinking aboot it. She took the spunks fae the mantel-piece and went oot intae the dusk o' the quiet nicht. What cracklin' there wis afore the rucks went intil a blaze! What a blaze! The sicht o't took the fullness awa' fae Rose's inside; she felt licht and empty, she had nae mair anger. She wasna even feart fan she heard their shouts and runnin' feet; she waited for them, haudin' the box o' spunks still in her hand.

They aye mindit on Rose; the piano in the sitting-room was a livin' memorial o' her; only the farmers' wives, that Dykie's mistress was friendly wi', kent hoo the piano was a memorial. Dykie's mistress tell't them.

'No, she wasna jilet; she was simple, ye see. She's in some hame for that kind o' craitturs; bit fa wad hiv thocht a quate, gumption-less thing like yon wad hae haen sic an idea? She wis heirt-lazy, of coorse. I'd aye maist o' the work tae dae mysel'. The threshin'-mill wis comin' neist day, an' Rose wis that feart o' a little extra wark. Still an' on the rucks war weel insured. Atween you an' me we got mair aff the insurance than ivir we wad hae got for the oats; it wis a licht crap. I got a new piano oot o't, onywey.'

PART II

SELECTED EARLY POEMS

A SCARLET GOON

O the regret as a body growes auld!
I wad hae likit a scarlet goon
an’ a desk o’ my ain ’neath the auld, grey Croon.
But I nivir wun nearer the College airts
than a Sunday walk doon the cobbled toon.
King’s gaithered a’ its ain wise thochts
intae its ain grey fauld.
Bein’ young, I grippit on tae the daftest thocht of a’,
feel, feckless, wi’ naething to ponder on
but a tryst tae be keepit by Brig o’ Don.
Gin I’d hae worn a scarlet goon
Fat wad I ken?
Mair or less than I ken noo
livin’ mang men wha nivir heard o’
Aristotle, or Boyle, that made a law,
or Pythagoras, an’ sic like chields
wha’s wisdom’s gie heich up, and far awa’.
My Alma Mater’s jist the size o’ a’ the fowk I ken,
An’ jist the colour o’ their thochts,

grey whiles wi' mole-hill griefs that mak'
true mountains;
gowd harled wi' sma' lauchs and greater humour;
black wi' humphy-backed despair;
alowe wi' hopes that whiles come true
but mair than often find slow beerial there.
And whiles it's green,
For jealousy torments even lads
wi' nae letters ahint their names.
A' that I ken.
—But still, I'd hae likit a scarlet goon,
an' a desk o' my ain 'neath the auld grey Croon,
Learnin' a little from the wise.
Dancin wi' gowden sheen,
Lauchin' wi' care-free eyes,
—Instead o' lifting tatties in mornin's glaured and cauld.
—O the regret, as a body growes old!

---

alowe—ablaze glaured—made muddy, slippery

BLAEBERRY WOOD

Our Street had a face I did not know, in the
early morning light—
Not tired and hot and crowded, as it had looked
last night.

I came upon it unawares,
Before the day, with pressing cares,
And noise and dust and weary heat,
Unceasing tramp of hurrying feet,
Had caught it up. Night must have lent some magic
to Our Street.

And deep in me arose an eagerness
That I must dance to show my happiness.
But there was never an eye to see
This fun and gaiety of me.
Yet I knew someone understood.
'Twas all because of Blaeberry Wood.
Down our Close, up Murdoch's Wynd,
I left the East-end far behind,
And now must walk with quiet feet
Along West Road—the rich folks' Street,

With villas standing stiff and prim,
Each with its garden neat and trim.
They all seemed very much the same
But for a number or a name.
And yet their dust-bins in a row
Made my heart beat, my eyes to glow.
How carefully I'd search each bin,
Excited, plunging headlong in
For a broken doll or a coloured tin.
Sometimes a dog would come as well,
And prowl around, and smell and smell.
Wagging his tail, to the next he'd run,
As if he, too, found dust-bins fun.
Life at the child must often smile—
The rich folks' dust-bins a Treasure Isle!
And now the long straight country road
With my dust-bin booty for my load.
Here was the wood. Within I flew
To a secret spot that alone I knew,
Where hyacinths, wild and wet and blue
In their hundreds and hundreds grew.
There on the wet grass, on my knees,
I pressed my face in the heart of these.
No smell I know is half so good
As the hyacinth tang in a morning wood.
I ever saw them with new eyes.
My heart was quick to meet surprise.
So now I set to work with a will.
'I think my pail will never fill.'
The rustling trees and the rising wind;
The town's left ever so far behind.

And the crackling twigs, and the bird-calls shrill;
The wood was never a moment still.
And now the droning of a bee.
Everything's busy round here—but me.
I just watch and watch the hole by the tree
For the rabbit that I was never to see.
The sun grows warm. The moss is deep.
I'd like to sink—and to sleep and sleep.
It's colder now. I think I'll call;
The world is strange when the shadows fall.
I'm not afraid, afraid at all;
But, all the same, I think I'll call.
Now where's my doll and flowers and tin?
What can I carry the whole of them in?
If I but could, if I but could,
I'd have carried away the half of the wood
Home in my arms. The foxgloves broken,
The hyacinths limp, are just a token.
Every bit of me is blue.
Hands, face, and knees, too.
But my heart has a vivid colour I know.
It's so warm inside me—a fire aglow.
So-long! So-long! It's been a treat.
On my way again with hurrying feet,
Half-glad, half-sad, back to Our Street.
I'll never grow too old to love Surprise,
Thank God! I still can see through a bairn's eyes.
A bygone trip, an enchanted wood—
A little girl who understood.

FIR WUD

Happit fae daylicht's cauld clarity.
Hidden the road.
An' here for lang
a yalla-yitie quietens the warld's steer,
an' mortal thochts,
wi' the lift o's sang.
Like velvet atween ma hot bare taes
the fir loam sifts.
Birstlin' things stick till ma claes
an' the foosty guff o' an ancient wud drifts
owre and bye.
If, forivir in this wud I jist could lie
an' tine ma thochts,
an' smell the resin, loam-filled air,

Happit—protected
yalla-yitie—yellow hammer
steer—bustle
Birstlin—completely dry
foosty—musty, mouldy
tine—leave behind
quine—young girl

an' watch the queer wud dirt gaither
tae battle on ma hair!
Sharpenin' draughts nip owre ma face.
Nivir sae wide awak', I shut ma een;
Syne, like a lustful quine,
gie a' masel tae the wud's embrace.

TO NAN SHEPHERD

Two hoors did haud oor years o' kennin' each
the t'ither's sel',
While words poored forth, swift burns in spate,
syne tint themsel's in the myrrh's thick smell,
We twa grew quate tae listen till oor thochts
gang loupin' through the wuds, and owre the
distant hills.
Jist aince we cried them back, and changed them
wi' each ither, like tokens,
Sayin', 'Keep mind o' that still river faur trees
glower lang an' deep at their reflections'.
Nor could the jostlin' fowk and noisy street touch for a
meenit oor communion.
Tho' I held oot a hand in pairtin',
I wisna aince my lane on the homeward track.
For, through myrrh's smell, past wud's tremendous
green,
My frien' just followed me, the hale wye back.

---

tint—lost my lane—alone

AUTUMN DYKE

A streetch o' sober dyke gairds a' the corn,
Like some auld-farrant chiel with-haudin' his
gowd-haired quines
Frae burstin' in flamboyant ecstasy.
An' a' the while they shak' their heavy tresses
An' reeshle in their laughter secretly.
Syne, farrer on, flauntin' the dyle intae obscurity
The hips an' haws afire, gleamin' wi' rain.
That Autumn nicht put blindness on tae me.
I'll niver see the lang stane dyke again.
In Spring an' Simmer, ay, in Winter, tae,
I'll see the lauchin' corn an' the reid hips
Weet wi' the rain.

---

auld farrant—old-fashioned   reeshle—rustle

PART III

EARLY RADIO WORK

ANYBODY'S ALLEY:

SOME MEMORIES OF A SCOTTISH CHILDHOOD

Announcer: This is the Scottish Home Service. We present 'Anybody's Alley' by Jessie Kesson, a memory of childhood.

Storyteller: 'Why, that's my dainty Ariel, I shall miss thee'. It's a far cry from Shakespeare and Prospero's dismissal of Ariel to a city slum called Murdoch's Wynd, and yet . . . I wonder . . . If I glimpse down the tunnel of the years to that same Wynd, it seems to me that Ariel did not belong to Prospero alone.

Annie Grigg (Elderly woman's voice): Anither pail o' water—my word, what a clivir quinie! An' ye've trailed it up a' this stairs yersel', bit wait you, I've a richt ba' for you—a great big ane. It's got bonny colours a' owre it an' it will nivir burst . . . You'll get it, ma quinie, you'll get it. Only I jist canna lay hands on it ae noo . . .

Storyteller: I never did get that ball—nor any of the other wonderful things Annie Grigg promised me—and yet, somehow I never lost faith in Annie—nor did I stop carrying her pails of water up three flights of stairs. My mother would laugh at Annie's promises and say, 'Annie wull nivir send ye awa' wi' a sair hert!' Nor did she. Annie lived in a wee room above us. She was a witch—but a good witch. Her hair was short and grey and curled round her head like a golliwog; her eyes were dark and twinkling; she smoked forever at a wee clay pipe. She took snuff—so that you would think the brown thing under her nose was a moustache; it wasn't; it was snuff.

Annie's attic fascinated me as greatly as Annie herself. I never once saw inside it. I smelt it! Annie was a lover of cats; a cat usually purred round her shoulders. I was quite sure that all the unburstable balls and golden-haired dolls that Annie promised me were somewhere in that attic, for Annie was a witch and would have given me the moon if she could have 'lain hands on it'.

Sometimes, though, usually on a Saturday night, my witch fell from her eyrie.

There was something terrible in the aspect of Annie lying in the lobby, her snuff-mill and her clay-pipe forgotten beside her—and her husband standing up in the eyrie swearing down at her. No one in the whole tenement seemed to realise the indignity of my beloved Annie's position—at least my frenzied cries, 'Come on, Somebody! Missis Grigg wull die!' went quite unheard.

Voices: Strawberry, Gooseberry, Apricot jam,
Tell me the name of my young man,
A—B—C—D—E—F—G
Strawberry, Gooseberry, Apricot jam.

Storyteller: When Annie did die, it was skipping time; and death affects a bairn's skipping. It was my first realisation of death. I knew people died, we used to race down to the bow of the Wynd to stare at passing funerals—but it was always other people who had died, not us—or ours—so when Annie died death became real. I thought if Annie could die my mother could die too. So I couldn't skip long—I was aye running up the Wynd into the lobby shouting up to my mother—(to the great amusement of the other tenants)—'Mam, wull ye nae die soon! Say ye winna die soon'. If my mother was busy, she would answer, 'For goodness' sake rin an' play. I dinna ken fan I'll die'.—Running away again, skipping for a wee while—

Voices: Strawberry, Gooseberry, Apricot jam . . .

Storyteller: Not able to skip very long because I was in suspense about this thing—death. Running up the Wynd to the lobby again, entreating, 'Mam, jist say this one time that you winna die soon!' The answer drifting down, comfortingly—'No, no, fat wad I dae dyin' soon?' Able to skip a long time because I had a mother who wouldn't die soon.

Voices: Strawberry, Gooseberry, Apricot jam,
Tell me the name of my young man.

Balaclava: My certes, ye little besoms! Bawlin' oot o' ye on a Sabbath!

Voices: Auld Balaclava free from sin
She'll go to Heaven in a corned-beef tin.

Balaclava: I'll corn-beef ye! They should be skint alive, the little vratches.

Storyteller: Balaclava was another of the Wynd's witches; we bairns were terrified of her. She would hobble down to the well muttering to herself—or laughing—a hideous, toothless laugh—terrifying because she laughed at nothing and to nobody. I had most fear of her; she lived in the room under us, and sometimes when I turned my mother's press into a caravan and trailed it across the floor, Balaclava would knock up with her brush, and the plaster would fly down from our walls at each knock. If my mother wasn't in the room, the moment became terror, I just waited for Balaclava to appear through the floor, complete with brush, grinning hideously.

If my mother was visible, Balaclava's knocking lost its fantastic dread. My mother killed it by vowing—'If that auld bitch disna stop knockin' the plaister aff oor wa's I'll gang doon an' brain her. We pay oor rent as weel's her'.

(Piper playing 'Inverness Gathering': fade for)

Storyteller: But no one in the whole Wynd had the enchantment of Paddy the piper. A pair of tartan trews and a Balmoral bonnet gave Paddy a grandeur possessed by none. At the first strains of his pipes we bairns were off behind him up the main streets, down the side streets—the Pied Piper hadn't more ardent followers. We felt a priority over the other bairns who joined in. A priority jealously guarded, swiftly asserted—'He's oor Paddy! He bides in the same Close as us!'

(Piper: fade up and fade down)

Reader: But she was beautiful,
Her beauty made the bright world dim.

Storyteller: Shelley too, is a far cry from Murdoch's Wynd, and yet I think his words could be applied to Poll. I didn't like Poll, but I liked to look at her. She wasn't tired and drab, she was dark-haired, bright-eyed, vivid: she wore a lot of jewellery and when she laughed her ear-rings shook and twinkled. It was difficult to avoid Poll. She stood forever at the bow of the Wynd—acting as a telescope—when anything exciting like a funeral passed or a fight took place. Poll's voice rang up the Wynd, 'Come on, you anes! Come on an' see this bonny big beerial!' or 'Come on! There's a barney at Hill Street! Come on quick. Here's the Black Maria.' No, I didn't like Poll. When I would emerge from playing in the refuse dump at the back of the Wynd, Poll, whose keen eyes missed nothing, would stare at me and say, 'Awa' an' wash yer face. Water's nae scarce an' soap's nae that dear.'

But the real delights of Murdoch's Wynd lay in the cries that the different seasons brought to its Bow.

Voices: Eily o Lo, lo lo, gies nuts.
Eily o Lo, lo, lo, gies nuts.

Storyteller: It was Halloween when that cry rent the streets round the Wynd. Bright, flare-lit Halloween. We bairns raced down the streets shouting that slogan. On this one night of the year the shop-keepers opened their hearts and threw on to the streets all the sweets and nuts we could scramble for. It was a mixed pleasure; only the fittest survived the wild scramble amongst the cobbles. I would be scrambling and greetin' at the same time—not quite sure if I was greetin' because the big loons stole my nuts or because they stood on my bare feet—a bit of both, I think!

Man: Canaries for woollens! Balloons for rags!
Flying canaries! Coloured balloons!

Bring oot yer jars. Rin hame for rags.

Storyteller: That cry too was usually the signal for tears. Somehow I could never convince my mother that one of her blankets was a fair exchange for a yellow, paper canary that flew on the end of a stick. 'A gweed blanket for a bit paper,' she would say, 'Nae the day, quinie.' And so I would hover beside the canary-man's cart crying bitterly and informing the street in general, 'Bit it's nae a bit paper, it's a canary.'

Voices: Fa saw the nursery-weeders?
Fa saw them ga-in awa'?
Fa saw the nursery-weeders?
Marchin' doon bi Balahaugh.
Some had shoes and some had stockings
An' some had nane ava'
Fa saw the nursery-weeders?
Fa saw them ga-in' awa'?

Storyteller: Summer brought that cry. Then the Wynd was deserted, for the summer through every bairn from eight years upwards went to weed and pull cabbage-plants at the local nursery. I was never quite sure if I was weeding carrots or young trees; nor had I much time to think—a kick from the weeder behind was a signal to scurry to the next stage. Across from the nursery was the Lunatic Asylum; when we had a moment to relax, we didn't use it; we climbed the nursery dyke and glowered over at the inmates. An angry foreman brought us back to earth—and our work—by shouting: 'Ye're nae use here, ye've pull't oot half o' the carrots. Come doon oot o' there.'

But on a Saturday afternoon the asylum, foreman,

carrots and cabbages were all forgotten in the excitement of having a pay envelope with your name on it and eight and threepence inside it, racing home, gripping on to that envelope like grim death, not opening it for anything in the world, till the proud moment when you gave it to your mother. I aye got the threepence to myself, so Saturday afternoon took on a golden, endless aspect. It took a lot of imagination to get the most out of threepence before I changed it into six ha'pennies and then into a lucky bag, a lucky tattie, a ginger-bread man, a ha'penny's worth of caramels and a penny for the pictures.

Reader: Yet bring I to my days an eager joy,
A lusty love of life and all things human!
Still in me leaps the wonder of a boy,
A pride in man, a deathless faith in woman.
Adventure beckons through the summer gloaming,
Oh long and long and long will be the day
Ere I come homing!

Storyteller: That's how it is. Your true gamin never quite outgrows his aliveness. Little tokens symbolise a life for him. I could find the four seasons of the year in a stunted beech-tree that somehow grew and flourished at the back of the rag-store in Murdoch's Wynd. When that beech-tree was green I knew it was Spring and Summer, when it was yellow it was Autumn, and when the beech-tree was nothing but a queer-shaped stick—it was Winter.

Money was scarce enough to be very joyous when we did have a penny to spend. And when we hadn't—then you never knew—anything could happen in

Murdoch's Wynd. I, for one, could never pass a street-brander without kneeling down and peering into its depths; queer things found their way into branders. If anything as big as a sixpence glinted in its depths, I would guard the brander for hours till an obliging passer-by lifted it for me. The lifting was on an honourable basis; I never claimed the sixpence as once having been mine; I claimed it because I saw it first.

And the Wynd had its own strange, hurting beauty, when the nights were drawing down and the chip-shop at the corner was lit up and was the only alive thing in the darkness; sounding good; looking good; smelling good; and the gramophone inside it playing

Gramophone: 'When You and I were Seventeen . . .'

Storyteller: And Vicky Stewart and Ethel Mutch, who were growing too old to play with us, would waltz together to the music under the street lamp, and for a moment we'd be caught up from our play to watch them—it was a long moment—for in that moment it seemed to us that the years couldn't pass quickly enough till the time came when we would be big enough to have curls in our hair, powder on our faces, and to be able to waltz to music—under the street lamp.

Gramophone: 'When You and I were Seventeen . . .'

Storyteller: That's why I'm glad I never broke my wand and dismissed Ariel—for now when I glimpse down the years, a slum becomes enhanced: its greyness shades from rose-pink to vivid gold, and people cease being people and tumble out in rich assortment—characters—from all childhood's storybooks.

THE CHILDHOOD

Male Reader: This then was my childhood. Alone
in the tall house, the lamp-lit rooms, the long
passages stealthy as nightfall.
Here, the years I recall are years
without time, condensed to one hour,
One everlasting moment; or that fall
out of time altogether, years that
flower into space—
And I am wounded by their outlived joy.

Highland Schoolmaster: So your name's Kernon. Daniel Kernon. You're from Glasgow. You're ten, are you?

Danny (Boy): Yes.

Schoolmaster: Yes what?

Silence

Schoolmaster: Yes what?

Silence

Schoolmaster: The word is 'Sir'.

Danny: Sir.

Schoolmaster: Say 'butter'.

Danny: Bu'er.

Schoolmaster: (Emphatically) BUTTER.

Danny: Bu'er.

Schoolmaster: The first thing I've always to teach you boarded-out children from Glasgow is how to say butter. And the only thing that does teach is this. Hold out your hand.

(Sound of tawse being applied. Fade up outside: country effects, and school just out, shouting, etc.)

Boy (Glasgow accent): Here, Kernon! that's no the wye to the woman you're boarded-oot wi's house; that's the main road. You go up the side road.

Danny: I'm going on the main road. I'm no steyin' here. I'm goin' back tae Glesga tae ma maw.

Boy: (Surprised) Hiv ye got a maw?

Danny: Yes.

Boy: How are ye boarded oot then?

Danny: The Green Lady took me. My maw went on the batter.

Boy: Dae ye ken the Garscube Road?

Danny (With first sign of warmth): I stayed in't, so I did.

Boy: So did I. Mind the Tollcross Picture Palace? I went ivery Setterday.

Danny: It was rer bit.

Boy: There's no picture palaces here, jist the church. Ye've tae go three times on Sunday. It gies me the pip.

Danny: I'm no goin'. I'm goin' back tae Glesga tae my maw.

Boy: It's no worth tryin'; we've a' tried it. Ye just get catched and then ye get a beltin'. I'll have tae dash, I've a lot o' work tae dae fan I get up to my auntie.

Danny: Does your auntie stay here?

Boy: No. I'm boarded oot as well, in that house beside the bridge. Most o' the kids here are boarded oot. We've got to call the woman we stay with 'auntie', but they're no like real aunties.

Danny: I'll no call yon wumman 'auntie', never. I hate her. She gies me brose and oatcakes, it's no grub. It's—it's hens' meat!

Boy: I'm aff—go up the cart-rut, mind!

(Danny throws himself down behind a broom bush—he's only ten—strange and homesick. He cries)

Danny: I hate her, I hate this place. I'm wantin' my maw!

(Fade)

Daniel (As a man): I remember lying hidden in the darkness of that broom bush. I cried then as I had never cried before—or since. I felt the taste of the sand on the ground in my mouth. But that cry helped me. As my boarded-out childhood wore on, I could even bring myself to call the woman 'auntie'. She died, when I was fifteen.

She was the first dead person I'd ever looked upon, and as I looked, I had no feeling of sorrow, or pity, or loss. I felt cold towards her dead. As cold as she had felt towards all her boarded-out children while she had lived. She was never actively bad to any of us; what she did was to take our whole childhood away from us with her two hands; withered, grasping hands, for I can never remember her as anything but an old, dried-up woman, too far away from her own youngness to have any understanding of ours.

(Fade in)

Kate (A boarded-out girl about thirteen): Danny! Danny!

Wait for me. Don't be going so fast. She'll get the breeze up if we don't all come home from the church together.

Danny (As boy): Hurry then. We're late as it is: we shouldna have played so long at the brig.

Kate: Wait then! I've got to go into the barn and take off the corsets and hide them till tomorrow.

Danny: Corsets? What things are that?

Kate: Och, stays.

Danny: Oh I know what stays are! My maw used to throw hers at the fit o' the bed: we used to take the iron things out of them and ping each other wi' them. You can take them off in the house, but.

Kate: No I can't; they're her stays. I—I didna really steal them, Danny, I just took a loan of them. I need stays now, but she says the parish won't give stays, and she'd never buy them for me herself.

Danny: Mean Bitch. Hurry up, then. Hide them; I'll wait here at the barn door.

Old Woman: (Crying at short distance) Daniel! Kate! What is it that you're doing in the barn?

Danny: Nothing. We're coming. *(To Kate)* Hurry, Kate, she's calling!

Old Woman: Daniel! Kate! Are you hearing me speaking to you?

(Fade in: Danny and Kate have arrived in the house)

Old Woman: Kate, what were yourself and Daniel doing in the barn?

Kate: Nothing—we—we just had a look to see if there were any eggs.

Old Woman: That's a lie. You know I never allow you to be gathering eggs on the Sabbath. Tell me the truth. What were you doing? If you're going to lie to me I'll write tomorrow and report you to the Glasgow Authorities.

Kate: (Upset) I—I—It was the corsets, your corsets, I just took a loan of them. I need corsets.

Old Woman: Go upstairs to your bed at once, Kate, and ask God to forgive you for being a deceitful, wilful—

Danny: She isn't—she told you the truth! She—

Old Woman: And you go to bed too. *(Mumbles half English, half Gaelic)* mi si dhu si mara. It's an awful bad girl that's in it, mi si dhu . . .

(Fade)

Daniel (As man): Once a month I was allowed to write a letter home to my mother in Glasgow. It was never a real letter, because she had to read it first. I can see her yet—peering like an old owl in the dim light of the paraffin lamp, reading what I had written for her benefit, and myself sitting there in the dark corner bursting with all the things inside me that I had wanted my mother to know.

Old Woman: So you've finished your mother's letter already, Daniel; you never tell her very much, do you? *(Reads)* 'Dear Mother, I hope you are well. I am fine and happy here, so don't you worry; the cow had a calf. I feed it out of a pail. Write soon.' Yes, well, that will be all right. I'll post it with the mail.

(Fade)

Daniel (As man): But it wasn't all right. Especially in winter. Winter up in those hills was always so terrible. And I seemed to see that winter rushing down the hill-side until it overwhelmed the Garscube Road itself. With the first sign of ice that lay in the cart-ruts and spread itself over the loch, I wanted to run up to the house and write down there and then to my mother:

Danny (As boy): Dearest Mother, Watch your feet on the ice: be sure and watch especially if you've got a drink in. I've so many things to tell you. Things you never knew, things I've been learning. I never learn a new song or a new poem or see a new thing but I save it all up in my mind to tell you about when I came home . . .

(Fade)

Daniel (As man): And because I couldn't write it, I prayed it. I could pray as I dug the frozen turnips out of the field, or boiled the hens' pot, or coming home from school with a shouting crowd of bairns. I could pray it anywhere, even in the middle of the auntie's Grace—while she thanked God for our brose and skimmed milk and for her own plate of ham and eggs.

(Fade in)

Old Woman: For what we are about to receive, make us humble and thankful, and pardon our sins for . . .

Danny (As boy): (Urgently) Don't let my maw slip on the ice, ye ken fine I'd aye tae help her along the slippery pavements on Setterday night—so dear, dear God, you watch her now.

(Pause)

Daniel (As man): The house was like the woman herself—it was tall and gaunt and gloomy. It had never the warm glow of firelight or lamp light, for she begrudged both peats and paraffin. It was a mean, spare house; we children would be sitting memorising a bit from the Bible—and the only sound in the house at all was her complaining voice.

(Fade in)

Old Woman: Ochone, ochone. Who was it that was heaping the peats on the fire? Was it you, Daniel? And the peats so scarce and the winter so long. And och you'd better all be going upstairs to your beds. The lamp's going down and we mustn't be using too much paraffin. But not so fast, boy: you haven't said your verse from The Book.

Danny (As boy): 'The Lord is my shepherd, I shall not want. He leadeth me by the still waters. He maketh me to lie down . . .'

(Fade)

Daniel (As man): 'To lie down'. The only sweet place in that whole house was my own attic at the top of it. It smelt fresh and sweet like the byre when it was newly strawed. It had a small, sloping window which only let me see one star at a time. When the window was open I could sometimes hear the sheep bleating on the hill at the back of the house, and I would remember the desolation that hill had for me the first time ever I saw it when we helped to round up sheep for the dipping. I had never seen a hill before. Nor have I since seen one more terrible. It rose sheerly out of the Loch. It was full of deep, narrow gulleys, and covered with great rocks.

The other boarded-out Glasgow bairns had become used to the hill, but maybe they still remembered their own first terror of it; at any rate they made quite sure I wouldn't escape it! I couldn't bear it. I ran away from them and hid in one of its rocks. Long and long I hid till the darkness came down and the wind rose and the desolation came over myself and the hill, a desolation I never quite lost.

(Fade in—sound of wind, an odd sheep bleating, and the peewits going home. The sound of the wind changes into the voices of the other boarded-out children initiating Danny into their own remembered terror of the hill)

First Boy: And if your foot slips, Kernon, just one wee slip—

Second Boy: You'll land right intae the Loch!

Third Boy: The Loch hasna a bottom—

First Boy: A boarded-out kid slipped intae it years ago!

Third Boy: They never found his body.

Second Boy: A shark ate it—

First Boy: It wisna a shark—it wis thousands o' fishes!

Second Boy: I can jump off this rock tae the yin on the other side o' the gulley!

Third Boy: So can I. So can I!

Second Boy: You jump it, Kernon.

First Boy: You're yella! Ye canna.

Second Boy: Kernon's yella! Fearty!

Boys Voices: (Intermittently through noise of wind—as wind) A shark ate him . . . The Loch hasna got a bottom . . . You jump it, Kernon . . . just one wee slip! He's yella! You jump it! Kernon's yella! Yella! A shark ate him . . . You jump it . . . *(Climax voices into high wind)*

(Fade)

Daniel (As man): But that was a fear that lay in my remembrance only. There was another fear that was always with me, like a dim, nagging ache. Then suddenly it would leap out of its hidden-ness. A cold sweat would come out on me, and I couldn't even see the rooshacs that Kate and I would be picking out of the pit. I couldn't see anything but the fear that stood in front of my eyes.

(Fade in)

Kate: (Anxiously) Danny! Danny! You're putting all the big potatoes into the hens' pot! She'll go mad! It's the rooshacs we've got to pick!

Danny (As boy): (Absentmindedly) It's the trams, Kate. Maybe she won't see it coming; maybe it'll run her down!

Kate: Who?

Danny: My maw.

Kate: I once saw a tram fall over: you should have heard the folk screaming.

Danny: Did they die?

Kate: Some of them.

Danny: (Urgently) I get so feart, Kate. I'm so feart my maw will die before I get back to her. I—I didn't use to get feart when I steyed wi' her. It was as if nothing could happen to her because I was there. Now I keep minding on all the things that could happen to her; the fights on the stair-heid in the dark. She'll maybe get killed in a—

Kate: (Who means to be comforting but is very practical) She'll no get killed in a stair-heid fight, Danny—she'll only get her heid split.

Danny: Could she die wi' that?

Kate: No, they'd bandage it up in Oakbank.

Danny: It's the time, Kate! The time I've to wait before I get back to her! I wish I could catch a year in my hand and shake it, and shake it, till it hurried past.

Old Woman: (Crying from distance) The hens are after screaming their heads off with hunger! Aren't you finished picking the rooshacs yet?

Danny: (Lower voice) It's queer that she never dies. She's old enough to be dead!

Old Woman: (Distant) Don't be fooling around there! Get the hens' pot filled. And make haste with it, make haste!

(Fade)

Daniel (As man): 'Make haste!' My last year of childhood did just that. It was so swift in its going. And for all that my heart cried out to be back in the small street off the Garscube Road with my mother, my mind knew that this was the last year, the last chance. It would have to store up the things I'd never see or learn again. All I did, all I saw in that last year, took on a terrific, hurting significance. Even now it comes leaping out of my mind.

(Fade in)

Old Woman: And not a single turnip have you taken to the cow this night—just running like a mad thing on the hill you were. If it wasn't that you're to be singing in the church tonight I'd send you straight to bed: it's the bad, disobedient boy you are! And you to be singing in the church too!

(Solo boy: paraphrase on the Lord's Prayer)

Father of all we bow to Thee
Who dwell'st in Heaven adored.
But present still through all the years
The everlasting Lord.
From day to day we humbly own
The hand that feeds us still.

(Fade)

Daniel (As man): And, as I sang that in the quiet, crowded kirk, I didn't feel bad or disobedient. I saw the 'auntie' sitting there, straight and stiff, and the other boarded-out bairns, and all the other 'aunties', and I remember wanting to sing it; to sing it so that the hardness and stiffness would leave their faces. But when I came to the last verse I wasn't caring what their faces looked like. I didn't see them. I was remembering why I'd been 'running on the hill like a mad thing'; it was because of the last verse of the paraphrase. The words of it made me want to run up the hill, higher and higher—

(Last verse of paraphrase)

Forever hallowed be Thy name
By all beneath the skies.
And may Thy Kingdom still advance
Till Grace to Glory rise.

(Fade)

Daniel (As man): I looked on each day, event, place, in that year as if I were looking on it for the last time, and I was never out of trouble for not seeing and doing the ordinary things that I should have seen and done.

(Fade in)

Old Woman: Wherever has that boy got to now, Kate? He hasn't gathered a bit of kindling for the morning fire.

Kate: He's down by the way of the Loch, I think.

Old Woman: What can he be doing there? And the water pails are empty! Not a drop of water!

(Fade)

Daniel (As man): But there was! All the water in the world! That's why I'd gone to the Loch. I'd gone so often before, but I never really saw it till the day we learned to sing 'The Meeting of the Waters' in school.

(Small choir of children)

There is not in the wide world
A valley so sweet
As that vale in whose bosom
The bright waters meet.
O the last rays of feeling
And life will depart
Ere the bloom of that valley
Shall fade from my heart,
Ere the bloom *(Fade)* of that valley . . .

Daniel (As man): Our hill burns, brown foaming things, all ran down to the Loch. And for all that a burn in spate is an angry thing, there they were, hundreds of them, leaping into the great quiet Loch—and neither joy nor sorrow at their coming showed on the Loch's face. How it would sometimes take the steamers and toss them about, till there was nothing left but the fear in the heart of a small, watching boy, that the steamers would turn over and disappear.

I saw the meeting of the waters so often after that, that I could have counted the flowers that grew on the hill by the Loch. I knew each stone. My hands became scarred with grasping the bracken. I discovered that the primrose cheats the eye: only its flower was softer than velvet, sweeter than any mortal thing. Its leaves were rough and hairy and ugly. I knew that foxgloves had a smell—bitter it was, like the poppy's smell. The other boarded-out bairns sensed I knew it. I had no chums. I just never found the companion that was so companionable as solitude. They misunderstood it till I bled their noses!

(Fade)

First Boy: C'mon, we'll play 'Hoist the Green Flag'.

Second Boy: Will you be on oor side, Kernon?

First Boy: Don't be daft—you know Kernon never plays. He's too busy pickin' floories—he's a Jessy!

Second Boy: Kernon's a Jessy! He canna even run. Jessy!

Danny (As boy): (Quietly) Say that again.

(Silence)

I'm no' a Jessy! I'm no'! I'm no'! I'll pit the loaf on you a'.

Daniel (As man): Long ago when I'd cried I'd known what sand tasted like. After that fight I knew what blood tasted like, thick and warm like milk fresh from the cow. And I wasn't frightened at that moment—nor indeed ever again—for I wasn't fighting for myself. I fought for the hill and all that grew on it. I fought jealously, because the other bairns had come barging in on my secret place, and had not understood it. After that I was happy, I lost need of any personal affection at all from the 'aunt'; her coldness skimmed over me, and it didn't hurt me any more. I even lost need of the near memory of my mother. I belonged so fully to my own mind, to the brave words I learned in school, to the things my eyes saw, to the music my ears heard.

(Song—'Rise and Follow Charlie'—male singer. Sung not concerted but as if from memory)

On dark Culloden red with gore
Hark, hark they shout 'Claymore! Claymore!'
No more we'll see such deeds again,
Deserted is each highland glen.

(Keep song behind Daniel's voice)

Daniel (As man): And there I would be, so often on the hill, with the grand music in my mind. And, though I was small for my years, I, there and then, quite alone, fought all Scotland's past battles for her—she never lost a battle with me to help her. Nor Greece neither! For I was learning about the wooden horse of Troy. So intense a learning it was that some days I didn't even see the hill.

I saw nae the gowan:
I saw nae the fern.
The ae leaf I gliskit in the mornin's dule
Was my wee Latin book,
The lang mile tae schule.
And, clamberin' up the hill hame
Wi' Virgil in my loof
Troy worked sae greatly in my wame
tae pit it tae the proof.
I wud hae made a wudden horse
oot o' ilka aiken tree.
And cut the rowans intae spears
For the sake o' Chivalry!

And, strangely enough, it was singing that made me realise that Kate was growing up too. She even played with a certain seriousness.

(Fade in:
Children—singing game)

The wind, the wind, the wind blows high,
The rain comes dashing from the sky,
Kate McKenzie says she'll die,
For her lover in the rolling sky.

She is handsome, she is pretty,
She is the girl of the golden city.
She has lovers one, two, three,
Come and tell us who they be.

(Lighthearted but argumentative discussion by children, then take up last chant)

Andy Ainslie says he loves her,
All the boys are fighting for her.
A whip and a whip and away they go
Off to London heigh heigh ho!

Daniel (As man): It was a queer, troubled phase we were passing through, this almost physical pain of growing up, terrified that one would laugh at the other. And I did laugh on the day that Kate fixed her long plaits on the top of her head, looking something like the old 'aunt' herself.

(Fade in)

Kate: What like does that look, Danny? I can never see myself properly. The 'aunt' hates me looking in the mirror.

Danny (As boy): It's—it's not bad—*(Bursts into laughter)* But oh, Kate, you look so funny! You're like an old woman.

Kate: (Peeved) Well, that's what like I'll look when I am a woman!

Danny: You'll be a sight then if you look like that!

Kate: You're not such a beauty yourself, Danny Kernon.

Danny: It's different with boys; they don't have to be beautiful.

Kate: I'd like to be beautiful. I remember my sister. She looked awful when she came home from her work. Her knees looked red over the top of her wellingtons. And her hair was all screwed up in curlers. But after she'd changed her working togs and put on her powder and lipstick, she looked so different, so pretty. And then we'd hear her boyfriend whistling from the foot of the close, and she'd rush out to meet him. I thought he was an awful looking jigger. I wouldn't have had him for anything—but she liked him. She thought he was the best-looking boy in the whole close. It's funny, isn't it? You don't like girls much, do you, Danny?

Danny: I like you not bad, but the rest are too giggly.

Kate: Do I really look ugly with my hair up like this, Danny?

Danny: No, not very. You don't look too bad, Kate.

Kate: Do you think Andy Ainslie would—

Danny: Andy Ainslie? He's daft. He can't even spell. His nose runs all the time. He's a bubblie bokie.

Kate: He's not! He's not! You're just jealous, Danny Kernon. You're just jealous.

(Fade)

Daniel (As man): And there were other symptoms . . .

(Fade in)

Glasgow Boy: I'll soon be seein' the last o' this dump, Kernon. Dae ye no wish ye were me? I'll be home in Glesga in six days.

Danny (As boy): You're lucky.

Glasgow Boy: Sure thing! Dae ye know this, they wanted me tae learn a trade! Tae be a joiner! Niver on your Nelly! I'm goin' back tae my old man: he's a bookie, he makes pots on the dogs. Have you ever seen a dug race?

Danny: No.

Glasgow Boy: You want tae see one then. They're stickin' oot a mile. You've seen nothing yet. Glesga in six days' time, and a fish supper! Dae ye know I've almost forgotten what a fish supper tastes like, but I'll make up for it in six days. And the barras! Did you ever pinch aipples off the barras?

Danny: Often. I could sure nip quick wi' them.

Glasgow Boy: Same here! The old wifies and the teachers think we're daft when we come here first, because we're no used wi' country ways. They'd look just as daft to us if they were suddenly landed in the middle o' Argyle Street. Can ye imagine the old woman I'm wi'? *(Mimics her)*

Ochone! Ochone! It's just wicked this traffic!
Ochone! Ochone! It's taking the feet from me.

(Both boys laugh)

Glasgow Boy: Never mind, Kernon! Your day's comin'. I'll gie the Tollcross and the barras your love!

(Fade)

Daniel (As man): My love. It didn't belong to the barrows any more. It belonged to things from whom I expected no affection—the things of the country, the bird and beast, yes, and the very clatter of the pails in the byre, and the smell of the byre itself. They wouldn't let me down, for they couldn't love me. I was safe with them. They would neither flatter me nor scorn me, nor turn away. They were there for ever and ever. I was safe with all those things undying.

And then my fourteenth birthday came round, and brought me down with a thump to the things I'd let hold of. How well I remember my boarded-out birthdays. They were days that leapt shiningly out of the years. My mother never forgot them. I used to waken early—indeed I never really slept at all on the night before my birthday, for praying that the Loch would be calm enough to let the boat in with my mother's birthday present. And even on my fourteenth birthday—though I was old enough to fight Scotland's battles for her—I was still young enough to be terribly excited about my birthday present.

There was no present, no letter, on my fourteenth birthday.

(Fade in)

Kate: But it will come tomorrow, Danny, you'll see. Maybe your maw's down with the flu or something.

Daniel (As man): Always Kate would say that, but it didn't come. Then the disappointment over the forgotten birthday left me in the growing anxiety over my mother. She never wrote all that month—nor the next.

(Fade in)

Kate: But she will write, Danny, she will. You'll see.

Daniel (As man): And yet she didn't write. I felt the nakedness of the agony of it showing on my face. Then it was that I hovered forever round the old 'aunt', and I would have given the whole world for a comforting, reassuring word from her.

(Fade in)

Danny (As boy): But my maw! Why doesna she write? Why? I'm feart something's happened to her. I'm feart that she's—

Old Woman: Och, don't be pestering me about your mother! You'll hear sometime. You'd better be finishing the hen-house—

Danny: (Urgently) But it's two months now, and she hasn't written. She hasn't answered any of my letters.

Old Woman: Well, well, she won't be caring about it as much as you are. Yourself and Kate can be taking the eggs down to the van.

Danny: But my maw! She must be deid. She'd have written if she wasna deid.

Old Woman: (Irritated) Don't be mixing me up in the counting of the eggs, boy—and don't be hovering round me always! It's getting on my nerves! I can't help your mother not writing. You'll be none the worse of that!

Danny: But my maw's maybe deid—and you don't care! You don't care—you don't help me! I wish you was deid. I wish it! I wish it. I wish it.

(Fade)

Daniel (As man): About a month later Kate and I stood in the barn watching the folk coming up the hill to the 'aunt's' funeral . . .

(Fade in)

Kate: Danny, you wished it! Mind, you wished it that day.

Danny: But it wasn't my wish that did it. She just took a stroke.

Kate: Are you sorry, Danny?

Danny: No. Are you?

Kate: No. I cried. I don't think it was because I was sorry. But I saw the cailleachs crying, and I just cried too. You didn't cry once.

Danny: I couldn't.

Kate: She felt so cold dead. I touched her.

Danny: She felt so cold living.

Daniel (As man): I remember watching the folk coming up the hill to the funeral, all of them old. For except for the boarded-out children there was no young folk on the hill at all. We heard them speaking among themselves.

(Fade in)

First Old Man: Well, it was a quick going, Angus.

Second Old Man: Indeed it was; but she'd been prepared.

Old Woman: God-fearing and Christian she was always.

First Old Man: Who do you think will get the croft?

Old Woman: They say she'd a tidy bit laid by.

Second Old Man: She was thrifty. Oh, it's you, Daniel and Kate! You'll be missing the 'aunt', I'm sure. It was a good thing she was spared to see you up.

First Old Man: She brought up a good many Glasgow children throughout her life.

Old Woman: You would have thought some of them would have come up for the burial, though. I don't see a one of them.

First Old Man: (Drily) Och, it's just the way of children to be ungrateful and forgetful. It's just as I was saying to you the other day . . .

(Fade)

Daniel (As man): But I knew that it was neither forgetfulness nor ingratitude. I saw the children, reflections of Kate and myself, small shadows hacking the turnips out of the snow; going east to the well for water, west to the barn for straw; seldom playing; laughing in whispers, sitting in dark corners learning the Bible. Never knowing active unkindness, and never once knowing what it was to be able to put their heads on the 'aunt's' lap and sob out the bewildering hurts of childhood. I saw them all, and I knew it was not forgetfulness that had kept them from the burial, but remembrance. Through the door we heard the voice of the minister.

Minister: Man has but a little while to stay on earth.
His days are like the grass.
The wind bloweth over it and it withereth away.

(Fade)

In my father's house are many mansions. If it were not so I would have told you.

(Fade)

We thank Thee who taketh the sting away from death.

(Fade)

As a shadow life is fleeting,
As a vapour so it flies.
For the bygone years retreating
Pardon grant, and make us wise.

(Fade)

(Sound-effect of moving train as background to this description)

Daniel (As man): The wheels of the train that bore me homewards to Glasgow kept time with my thoughts of the place I had left behind. It was near, and very dear to me in the moment of leaving it. Half of me was glad and excited at the thought of seeing my mother and the Garscube Road: the other half was regretful. Regretful for stones, for the Loch, for music, for words: all things that couldn't know of my regret. As the train raced through Glasgow's great, black outskirts, a lostness came over me.

(Train slows down and stops: station effects)

(Fade in)

Brother (Glasgow accent): (Warmly) Danny, son! My, I hardly kenned ye! Ye've grown, bit. It's great to—

Danny: My maw! She didn't write. Where is she?

Brother: (Quickly, ignoring question) Listen. What about a cup o' tea? Come on in tae the buffet. You're bound tae be needin't efter—

Danny: But where is she—my maw?

Brother: (Quietly) She's in hospital, Danny.

Danny: Is she—bad?

Brother: She's better there, son, she—

Danny: I want to see her.

Brother: I'd wait a day or two. Go easy, Danny. You'll—

Danny: But I want to see her today, just now.

(Fade)

Daniel (As man): What I saw lying on that hospital bed wasn't my mother. It was something that was blind, deaf, speechless. In that moment I lost all I had. The delight I'd stored up within myself in the years on the hill, dried up inside me. For my mother was the only person who could ever have shared it or understood it, without having set eyes on it.

My brother and I walked towards the Garscube Road. I felt numb, but my outer senses still went on working. I could hear what he was saying.

(Traffic sounds: not too loud)

Brother: It was a stroke that took her, Danny, sudden like. The doctor said she didna suffer. You're gettin' a start wi' my foreman in the shipyard, son. Keep your chin up: you're a man now.

(Fade)

Daniel (As man): I remember walking on, seeing nothing. Then the numbness left me for an instant. It was a foolish, quick thought that slipped into my mind, a bit of a song that Kate used to sing—

O the garden of Eden has vanished they say:
But I know the lie of it still . . .

In that moment I wanted to cry. I didn't. And the moment passed. The numbness came over me again. I started asking my brother about the shipyard. I was a man, now.

(Boys singing in background)

Yet it was not that Nature had shed o'er the scene
Her clearest of crystal and brightest of green.
'Twas not that soft magic of streamlet or hill
Oh no, it was something more exquisite still,
Oh no, it was something more exquisite still.
'Twas the friends the beloved of my bosom were near,
Who made every scene of enchantment more dear.
And who felt that the best charms of Nature improve
When we see them reflected in looks that we love
When we see them reflected in looks that we love.

WE CAN'T GO BACK

I HAVE lived in the country most of my life. The real, remote country, where a visit to the nearest city becomes a great event. Sixteen years of my life were spent as a farm-worker's wife.

I don't know exactly when I first made up my mind to change my way of life. I think it was a very gradual decision, beginning when I lived amongst the lonely hills, in a countryside which didn't even boast a train. The trains were always across the water, on the other side. I began to feel restless, to feel that life was passing me by, that the real world was reached by a train, not by a ferry boat!

When I finally did make up my mind to leave this way of life, my neighbours didn't take me seriously. 'Ta ta, then, Kesson', they said, with a laughter of voice which implied: 'But ye'll be back amongst us in three months. Ye'll never stick London. Ye'll be fair lost. It's a terrible big place, yon!'

Five years have passed since then. And so I feel that I never properly said goodbye to them, because I know now that I'll never be back living and working amongst them again.

It's not a question of not wanting to go back! Many a time as I stand squeezed for an hour and a half in the tube on my way to work in the rush hour, I remember with longing how I once had a whole hill to myself, and all the time in the world to walk over it. And if I did share that hill with some shepherd, the fact that he was unknown never turned him into a stranger!

'Aye, but it's another fine night, again.'

'It is that. We'll just hope it keeps up.'

Not only do I miss the communion of country people, I miss the material things too. Not a mean person, despite what the jokes say, I nevertheless break my heart when I have to hand tenpence over for a small turnip for my broth: the acres of them that used to lie around my door, just for the lifting, don't bear thinking about! The potatoes, the milk I used to lash out on the Collie dog. I still retain the country wife's conviction that these things should not have to be paid for—except, of course, by people unfortunate enough to live in towns! I still have not got kindly used to the idea of posting off my mortgage cheque every month. And I still stare on my electricity bills with disbelief, and remember my paraffin lamp with affection.

Why then, can't I go back?

I'm not quite sure, but I'm going to try and reason it out honestly. And incidentally, when we do try to be utterly honest with ourselves, we don't always emerge as nice people. Bearing this in mind, I hope you will bear with the not so nice person I may reveal myself to be!

I can't go back, because a farm-worker's wife had little part in the life of the community. I know there are the Women's Rural Institutes, and a great social boon they are too, to the often lonely country-woman. But in my time at least, the farm-workers' wives were the audience, in the main, and I just longed to be the performer instead. I've got that wish now, you see! Quite seriously though, it can be a most frustrating thing if one feels the capacity for giving, whether it be ideas or talents, and one has got nowhere to give them to!

Since coming to London, I have had the opportunity to use what talents I have. I still find my salary cheque incredible. It almost seems to me wicked, to be paid so much money for doing something one enjoys doing. Something that doesn't seem like work at all. I used to work at the threshing mill on the farm. For one hour's work, I was paid one shilling. And country listeners will agree, I think, that it's the hardest earned shilling in the world. You don't know which part of you aches most. And, if it's a mid-winter thresh, with the frost still on the sheaves, you don't know you've got fingers left. For one hour now, working at an institute for young people, I am paid at the rate of one pound, and I don't even know the hour has passed.

You can imagine the contrast this has made in our standard of living: what used to be luxuries are now everyday necessities. More, it's very heart-warming to walk down the main street of our suburb, knowing that one is buying one's own house, feeling that one is important in their job. That one is no longer 'Kesson, her in that cottar house on the hill, a nice enough body'; but 'Ma'm' now, 'the lady that lives at 46'.

And yet, and yet. I seem to have lost all the spontaneous joy that little, rare happenings used to give. Like the coming of the threshing mill itself, with its promise of a bit of extra money, spent on the purchase of a secondhand dressing table, maybe. It gave me much more joy than my new cocktail cabinet gave me. I often look around my living room, furnished in what I hope is contemporary style, and I remember the kitchen of my cottar house, its real fire of sweet, pungent wood, gathered from outside my door. Its homely smell of paraffin. Each bit that furnished it a real personal triumph with its own story. It seemed to belong to the kitchen, to be part of our family. Now, myself and my contemporary furnishings stare coldly at each other, like strangers. It required no great effort on my part to acquire them, and I feel they know that!

I think perhaps I've got to the core of the reason why I can't go back. It is our dreams and plans that make day to day living bearable. These dreams and plans are stronger in our youth, and in the places where our youth is spent, but we have usually got to go away to fulfil them. Once we have done so, there is nothing to go back for. There is nothing more to plan, little else to dream of. And so I stay and live with the reality. And it was never so good as the dream of it was! I share the Scottish poet's intense nostalgia:

London is fine, an' for ilk o' the lasses at hame
There'll be sixty here.
But the springtime comes an' the hairst—an' it's
aye the same
Through the changefu' year.

Oh, a lad thinks lang o' hame ere he thinks his fill
An' his breid he airns—
An' they're thrashin' noo at the white farm up on
the hill
In the Howe o' the Mearns.

PART IV

SATURDAY NIGHT

SATURDAY NIGHT

Cry Hallelujah in Ansell Street
For your souls' sake!
Where old men cluster round its stalls
Like sores brought out by heat.
Fumbling with radio parts and secondhand tools
For the joy of touch and feel,
Till in their attitudes so consecrated
Junk takes on quality of instant worth,
Though not of value.
The old men seldom purchase,
No more than Mrs Eck appears to sell,
Looming in large indifference
Amongst the cast off clothes.
There's no demand, she reckons, for dead men's shoes
Or Ladies' hand-me-downs,
What with Italian suede and sailcloth
Going to their heads:
There's no demand for anything of quality,
Mrs Eck confirms,
Nodding assurance to herself distorted

In the Cut Price grocer's window,
Along with OMO DOWN TODAY
And SUGAR SLASHED AGAIN.
Only the woman shouting Marguerites
Tenpence a Dozen!
Retains cool confidence,
Cutting the last bunch down to Sixpence!
With fine finality,
Knowing the day's full profit
Allows the night's last loss,
And gathering herself together with paper and twine
Takes one last look and makes for Fred's
Fried Fish To Carry Home.
Conscious the world is nigh its end,
Mr Breen, firefull and hellsure,
Startles the quiet,
Shouting a personal Christ. Walking the gutter,
Beheld by Mr Breen himself, just forty years ago
At Manchester.
They don't believe him quite,
The folk who have hung around the stalls so long
Loving the lazy lie, the leaping legend,
Laying the odds on miracles more complex,
Never in Manchester! Their minds protest,
Keep Him in Galilee,
Dim memory urges walking the waves.
Amen! Amen!
Gintsy, half-witted, follower of orators,
Street corner clown,
Breathless from chasing salvation's trumpet gleam
Down half a lifetime,

Acclaims its light again
Amen!
She might as well shout Fish!
Live eels today!
Drowning her cry in the oyster chorus,
Amen!
The old men glance upon her without eyes,
Pondering her image within their being,
The strange familiar.
Ah men.
The new creed echoes round their orbit.
Top Ten. Without commandment.
And the saints cha-cha-ing in,
Rocking their souls in the bosom of Abraham,
Confusing the ancients.
Tom Dooley for the tree tomorrow,
—'Reckon you're going to die'—
A kind of Christ
Outwith poor Mr Breen's provincial prophecy,
—'Hang down your head and cry'—

PART V

RADIO

FREE FOR ALL!

OCTOBER. The hopscotch hieroglyphics of Summer fading on the pavement of our street. And the Police a race to be wooed and won in October! For it was then that they clattered up the Wynds in pairs. Flashing their torches in dark corners. To unearth, and Take Down the names of children eligible for a Free Christmas Dinner. The 'I Spy' excitement the procedure had upon us!

'The Polis are taking down the names in Singer's Close! Me and Isa saw them! As sure as death!'

'Big Aggie went clean Mad! She told them to stuff their Free Dinners!'

'And her man threatened to put the head on the Polis!'

The long wait between names Taken Down, and the official presentation of tickets for the Chosen Ones! A wait, filled in by October's other symbols of Christmas. Crowding round the window of Higgins's corner-shop. With its lit-up bribe—'All paid Up Members of Xmas Club Will Receive Mystery Free Gift!' A bribe which held special fascination for me, since my family usually fell by the wayside, in the long weeks of sixpenny payments. All we ever landed with was a caddy of tea and a packet of dates! But those who knew would shout loudly and scathingly, 'It's just a Calendar! That's all you get for free from Higgins. A lousy old Calendar!' And accordingly, we would all be chased away from Higgins's window by Higgins!

The day arrived at last, for the Official Presentation of Tickets for a Free Christmas Dinner. Trooping off up to the yard behind the Courthouse. Anxiety heavy within us. Nothing was ever certain. And you still might be the Forgotten One! The Chief Constable striding through the yard, escorted by a Policeman. All eyes fixed on the Chief's long, white gloves. Then directed upwards to scrutinise the escort Policeman. Just to assess whether he was friend or foe of one's acquaintance!

'It's the Wales Street Bobby!'

'So it is! The red-headed Bobby from Wales Street!'

The excitement of recognition. And simply the excitement. Suddenly burying all former hatchets. For it was the kind of moment when any familiar face was worth a cheer!

'Hurray! The Good Old Wales Street Bobby!'

An acclamation which left the Policeman unmoved. A kind of betrayal. As he stood calling out our names in a voice which disowned any previous acquaintance with us!

Our names were called out in alphabetical order. Small distractions heightened the tedium:

'What colour are the tickets this year, Moswer?'

'Yella!'

'Hurray! Yella Tickets! They were Red last year!'

And how easy it was to confuse the alphabet in moments of waiting tension.

'They havena called my name out yet!'

'There's hundreds of names to be called out yet!'

'But I'm a B. They're at the Ds now!'

'So they are! Are you sure they took your name down for a ticket?'

'As sure as Death! You was with me! You saw them taking it down.'

'They've forgotten about you, then.'

The temporary disruption in relationships, which the official possession of a ticket for a Free Christmas Dinner caused! The attitudes of our parents affecting us, and dividing us into two separate kinds. Those who Accepted Charity. And those who didn't! Causing confusion in our games. Hitherto so rooted in ritual.

Stand and face your Lover.
Stand and face your Lover.
Stand and face your Lover,
As we have done before!

'You can't stand opposite me! Josie always stands opposite me for my Lover!'

'Josie can't then! She's playing with the Free Tickets now!'

And the War of the Kinds would flare up.

'Free Tickets! Free Tickets!'

'Snooty Noses! Snooty Noses!'

'My Maw says you're just a lot of Give Mes!'

'My Maw never pops our Grand-da's Pension Book!'

'No. She just lets you put your name down for a Free Ticket!'

Christmas Eve. The strain of it beginning to tell on us, as well as on our parents! It was an unwritten law, formed and enforced by us, ourselves. Till it became a Tradition, that we would sooner forgo the Free Christmas Dinner than attend it in the same frock which we wore the previous year. A law to be defended, not only against our own parents, but against a formidable combine of their onlooking neighbours!

'For the love of God! Stop deaving me about a new frock! Whiles, I think it would be less worry to just sit ourselves down to a drop of soup from a ham bone! Where am I to get the price of a new frock for ye?'

'Now! Look you here, Josie Donald! Your Mother has trampit the streets all day to get a new frill for the bottom of your Jean Ann's frock! She doesna know if she's got feet left!'

'Lizzie McKenzie's got a new frock!'

'Lizzie McKenzies's Father's no on the dole!'

'And Jean Menzies's got a new one!'

'No doubt! From one of your Tally Men that's never off their door-step! Do you want to get your Mother up to the eyes in debt?'

Christmas Day at last! Good humour restored all round. The whole town standing on its doorsteps to cheer us on our way to the Town Hall. Remembering little about the actual Dinner itself. But the gift of an orange, an apple, a bag of sweets, lingers in the mind. And the New Penny lights it up. Reckless and prodigal with all of them—except the New Penny. A curious, shining hostage to fortune, with the date of a New Year, not yet arrived, engraved upon it.

'Jean's lost her New Penny!'

'You can have my sweeties, Jean. I'm sick of them!'

'I'm not wanting your sweeties. I've lost my New Penny!'

'You should have watched it, Jean! You should have put it down inside your stocking. That's where I put mine!'

The highlight of our day started with 'Three cheers for the Pipers!' A thousand strong, we would form up behind them, and march through the streets of the town to Free Seats at the cinema. A procession in the mood to cheer everything, from the mounted Policemen, to a cat scuttling across the street for dear life. A procession accompanied by the running commentaries of our kith and kin, lining the pavements, to see us go by.

'Three cheers for the Flea Pit!'

'Watch out for Tom Mix!'

'And keep your eyes skinned for Pearl White. She's got Something!'

'Trust you to know what she's got, Jake Scobbie!'

The cinema still a novelty. And a wonder magnified because this was Christmas Day. Imagination and reality fusing. And emerging in one great voice of mutual counsel and warning, to the images, so taken to heart, on the screen.

'Mind out, Tom! The Bad Ones are ahint that Rock!'

'Look OUT, Tom! For God's sake, look out!'

'He's seen them!'

'Here's HER again! They'll kiss each other for ages. And Tom will be catched!'

'Cut the Kissing, Tom! The Bad Ones will be back! As sure as Death, they'll be back!'

The Great Day not yet at an end. Grimly holding on to the last moment of its ritual. Singing carols up at the Bandstand. Tired, but aware that Christmas, without its carols at the Bandstand, would have been as incredible as Christmas without its Free Dinner! Racing homewards. Next Christmas, a lifetime away. With only the New Penny to prove, now, that this Christmas had been at all! And our minds already turning to the next big event on our Calendar!

Rise up auld wife!
And shak your feathers!
Dinna think that we are beggars.
We're only bairnies out to play.
Rise up and give us Hogmanay!

'We don't sing that till next week!'

'I know! I know that fine! I was just minding about next week. We'll have rare fun!'

'It's still Christmas, though! It's Christmas till twelve o'clock!'

SOMEWHERE BEYOND

I

Narrator: But now was come a change; it would demand some skill and longer time than may be spared to point, even to myself, these vanities. And how they wrought . . . For something there was about me that perplexed th'authentic sight of reason.

It was only on the day I left the Orphanage of my childhood, for my first job as kitchen-maid at a local farm, that it struck me I might be homesick for the Orphanage; and though the actuality was to prove as sharp as the apprehension of it had been, I never thought I would return to the Orphanage—sacked from my job—and in disgrace with Mrs Thane, the Matron—a disgrace intensified because it was witnessed by a lady who was a stranger to me.

Mrs Thane: Mary. This is Miss Erskine.

Miss Erskine: How do you do, Mary?

Mary Carron: How do you do?

Mrs Thane: It's all thanks to this lady that the Trustees have decided to give you another chance, Mary!—a course in book-keeping and typewriting at a school in

Kingorm. Though if you concentrate as little on that as you did on your job, it would be a waste of Miss Erskine's time.

Miss Erskine: What went wrong in the job, Mary?

Mary: It wasn't the work—I didn't mind about the work—I did try. Every night when I went to my bed I lay thinking about how hard I was going to work next day—but when next day came, I would think about things so long that the time passed, and the work wasn't done.

Mrs Thane: It certainly wasn't!

Miss Erskine: What did you think about, Mary? What kind of thing—

Mrs Thane: Anything but the thing she should have been thinking of, I'm sure of that! I had to keep a pretty tight rein on her when she was here. She would have buried herself all day inside a book and let anybody else that liked get on with the rest of it. I don't know what you will make of her, Miss Erskine, but she was always a bit of a puzzle to me.

Miss Erskine: I think she's beautiful, Mrs Thane. She's beautiful.

Narrator: When time and tide stand still, place itself can petrify you within it. It seems that a part of me still stands captive in the Orphanage sitting-room, almost incoherently grateful for the first spontaneous nice thing anyone had ever said about me.

Mary: Miss Erskine, there's something—do you know it? I read it once. This is what it says: it's about a boy reading Virgil and he tells what it did to him:

Troy worked sae greatly in my wame
Tae pit it tae the proof;

I wud hae made a wudden horse
Oot of ilka aiken tree,
And slashed the rowans intae spears
For the sake of Chivalrie.

That boy felt able to do anything in the whole world—do you see?

Miss Erskine: Yes. I see. You like poetry then, Mary?

Mary: It's the thing I like best.

Mrs Thane: And it is just all that reading and daydreaming that's kept her mind off her work! *(To Mary)* But you'll have to liven up your ideas, Mary, now that you are getting another chance.

Miss Erskine: But she will, Mrs Thane—I'm sure she will.

Narrator: And so was I. I had no doubt of that. On the day I set out for the Hostel for Working Girls, which was to be my home during the next six months. The inscription on the door, 'Hostel for Working Girls', was not quite true in that Autumn of 1933, for the Home's girls who were working were of the fortunate minority. But I knew nothing of that on the day I arrived there, and met the Matron for the first time.

Matron: So you are Mary Carron, Miss Erskine's newest protégée?

Mary: Yes.

Matron: Well, it is to be hoped that her faith in you is justified. We want no airs or graces. On the contrary, you should be mindful of the charity that has been extended to you. You realise that?

Mary: Yes. I'm glad—

Matron: This is a Home for Working Girls. Girls who work for their living, who have neither had your opportunity of further education nor the benefit of your Orphanage upbringing. You must accept these girls on their terms. Not on your own.

Narrator: It took me some time to accept the girls on their terms. For my attitude, though imposed upon me, had been strongly imposed, not only by the Orphanage, but by a rural Presbyterian way of life. I hadn't realised how strongly, till my first encounter with the girls.

(Old piano being strummed in accompaniment to girls singing)

Don't know why
There's no sun up in the sky,
Stormy weather,
Since my man and I ain't together,
Keeps raining all the time—

Ginny: (In protest) Aw! Not again! Give us Bing! Let's have 'Please'.

(Starts in solo opposition to 'Stormy Weather')

Please
Lend a little ear to my pleas
Say you're not intending to tease
Tell me that you love me,
Please.

(She falls out of contest in awareness of Mary Carron)

Are you the new tart for the empty bed in the Basement?

Mary: I am—new.

Ginny: (To Pianist, loudly) It's the new tart for the empty bed in the Basement. *(To Mary)* Are you on probation?

Mary: (Not knowing what 'probation' means) I'm going to school—to a Commercial Class.

Ginny: Imagine that! She's going to school. That's a change.

Second girl, Pianist: This is no the High School for Girls, hen! It's at the West End of the town. You've come to the wrong place, hen. *(Returns to 'Stormy Weather')*

Life is bare
Gloom and misery everywhere,
Stormy Weather.
Can't get ma poor self together.
Keeps rainin' all the time—
The time.

Mary: (To Ginny) Is this all the girls in the Home?

Ginny: No! We're the ones that's on the dole. The Fish Yard and Factory workers will be in soon. *(Ginny now takes up 'Stormy Weather')*

Since he went away
The blues came in and found me.
If he stays away
Old rocking chair will get me.

Narrator: The two girls in the sitting-room were my own age, but I stood considering them filled with envy. They had sophistication, a quality of which I am as bereft now as I was on that day when I first recognised it in others. So that when the other girls came in from factory and fish yard, I began to wonder whether I had come to the wrong place.

(Sitting-room: Pianist and two singers continuing)

Can't go on
Everything I have is gone
Stormy Weather.
Can't get my poor self together

Keeps rainin' all the time
The time.

(Door almost bang-forced open)

Peg, Third Girl: (Entering) Hold that tiger. Hold the Tiger!

(Piano, singing, chorded to close)

Ginny: What's hidden up your jake, Peg,—herrings?

Peg: Me frock—the Model! Five bob down—two bob a week, and ten bob off because it's a wee thing shop-soiled. Not so's you'd notice though!

Ginny: You'll never get it over your jumper.

Peg: Aye I wull. It's only a wee thing shop-soiled. Wait till you get a load of this! It's got a touch of class, so it has—Wait till it hits you! This frock's going to knock all the sheiks in the Gallows-Gate for ten!

Ginny: It's a Bobby-Dazzler, Peg, so it is.

Pianist: It's stickin' out a mile, hen.

Fourth Girl: It just shows off all you've got!

Peg: Just you watch it flare out when I swing the corners.

(Singing, accompanying her solo dance)

Come on along and listen to
The lullaby of
Broadway.
The hipooray and
Ballyhoo
The lullaby of
Broadway.

Ginny: (Intruding through performance vehemently) You canna see the shop-soil at all, Peg. Honest to God, ye canna!

Peg: (Swirling to standstill—complacently, matter of fact) Of course ye don't see it. Because I'm keeping my arm stuck down my side all the time. It's just a wee fade down the side, you see.

Ginny: (Dismayed) But you'll never be able to swing it, Peg. No with your arm stuck down your side all the time.

Peg: Sure I can swing it. You saw me swing it.

When the Broadway Baby says
Goodnight
It's early in the
Morning.
Good-night, baby,
Good-night—
Baby
See you in the morning.
Good-night Baby—

Ginny: What's up with the new dame's dial?

Peg: (Advancing towards Mary Carron) Listen you, whoever you are. What's up with your clock? If you're trying to take the rise out of me, you'll laugh with the other side of your dial! Because I'm going to land you one on the kisser.

Mary: It's just—it's just the new frock. It looks so funny with your curlers rattling and your big sea-boots on.

Peg: Oh yeah? *(Approaching near but very quietly—examining Mary Carron)* Have you ever taken a gander at yourself? If you havena, take one, quick. Because if I looked like you, I'd do myself in. Honest to God I would. I wouldna be found dead in them—*(words fail her)*—bloody rompers of skirts you've got on. *(Laughter from observing girls dying down)*

Mary: I'm sorry. I didn't mean it like that. It will look

lovely when your curlers are out and your boots are off. It's the loveliest dress I've ever seen close-up.

Peg: (Disarmed into surprise by the unexpected) Wha's your name anyhow?

Mary: Mary Carron.

Peg: Where do you come from?

Mary: Skene.

Ginny: Where about is Skene? I've never even heard of it.

Mary: It's in the country.

Ginny: (Heavy satirical surprise) The country? You don't say! Not that place where all the sheep and cows and things are? *(To other girls)* We'll have a barney! *(To Mary Carron)* Come on, hen. Come in amongst us. Down here on the couch and tell us all about it.

Peg: Can ye dance, Mary?

Mary: Not tangos and things. But I can do all the country dances. Strip the Willow and Eightsome Reels.

Ginny: Imagine that! She can do Eightsome Reels. Show us how to do an Eightsome Reel, hen. Come on. We're all dying for to see one. *(Appeals to others)* Sure we are? *(General assent of others)*

Mary: I can't show you. It needs eight dancers and there's no music.

Ginny: That's nothing. We can give you tune.

Girls: (Giving tune to their own words)

Aunty Mary she had a canary
Up the leg of her drawers
When Geordie Dudd made a grab at her—

(Girls dissolve in laughter. Laughter dies down)

Ginny: Tell us, Mary, had ye a sheik in the country?

Mary: A lad, you mean?

Peg: Aye, that's it. 'A lad'. Had you got one?

Mary: I could have had one.

Ginny: Why for no, then, hen? Was ye feart?

Pianist: Was he mustard?

Ginny: You know—hot stuff.

Peg: What she's getting at, hen, did he ever try you on?

Mary: (Aware now that they are taking the mickey, and angry) No. We were decent. Us in the country. We didn't swear and we didn't smoke, and we wouldn't have been allowed to speak to the like of you. If you lot ever landed in the country, you'd just look as daft there as I look here. You'd run for miles from the 'sheep and cows and things.'

Ginny: (Completely taken aback) Well! Is my nose still on my face?

Peg: So that's our new bed-mate.

Pianist: She says she's going to school.

Ginny: Maybe she's one o' they students that sometimes study us. You know the kind. *(Mimics)* 'Would you like to tell something about it? It sometimes helps to tell somebody, you know'.

Peg: (Shortly, astringently) Like Hell, it does. No, this chat's too young for that game.

Pianist: (Taking up notes of 'Stormy Weather' again, complacently) She's all yours, Ginny. Thank God I got a shift out of the basement dormitory. *(Fade Pianist)*

Narrator: Down in the basement dormitory I stood indulging in a technique which I had perfected in the Orphanage—that of bringing both eye and mind to concentrate so hard on one image, that all others were blotted out. I stood staring out of the window at a pram without a hood in the back-green above. 'I should be happy here', I thought, staring. 'It's like the Wynd at home. And I know it.' But I was beginning to feel some subtle change in myself. I disliked the dormitory because it had neither the dirty abandon of my attic at home, not the clean, clear-cut institutionalism of the Orphanage. I was standing absorbing the dormitory when the door opened.

(Door opens and closes)

Connie: (Shop Assistant, and superior in her own opinion to the other girls) You must be our new bed-mate. On probation.

Mary: No.

Connie: What's so different about you, then? Most of them here are. Seen any of them yet?

Mary: One called Ginny. She's bonnie, isn'y she?

Connie: She'll pass for looks. It's when she opens her mouth that she gives the game away. She's as common as cat's dirt. She's on probation for—

(Door slammed open)

Ginny: For what, big mouth? On probation for what? *(Turning to Mary)* I'll tell you for what myself, hen. Just so you get it straight.

Connie: (Nervously) Decent folk don't listen behind doors.

Ginny: Skip it. I'll tell the new tart myself. I'm on probation for helping myself to frocks. It wasn't a fur coat though, hen. I haven't got a fur coat. But if I ever get one it won't be the way Connie Clart here got hers. My Probation Officer hasn't given me a list of streets I mustn't be seen on.

Connie: I'm asking a shift upstairs. I'm going to ask for a move out of here.

Ginny: And we won't cry when you get it, hen. We'll throw a party, but I'll tell you this much; if you ever cast up my probation again, I'll brain you, you knock-kneed, puddin'-faced, Lady Muck.

Matron: (Approaching) What's going on down here now? What's all the arguing for?

Ginny: It's her. Her there—Connie Clart.

Matron: Connie who, Ginny?

Ginny: Well, her. 'You'll get a chance to live it down,' my Probation Officer said when she took me here, but she didn't know about Big Mouth there.

Matron: That's enough, Ginny. That's quite enough. Now get upstairs to the sitting-room all of you. Mary Carron—did they allow you to sit on the bed in the Orphanage?

Mary: No.

Matron: We don't allow it in here either!

Narrator: 'Maybe I'll really belong in school,' I thought. But when I did return to school I felt as out of place there as I felt in the Home. Nor did the fault lie with my class-mates, but in myself in trivial, baffling inadequacies. I couldn't find the right words when the girls in my class invited me to their homes. I wanted to blurt out outrageous things, not so much to shock my hosts as to prove to them that I did know about other things even if I didn't know about tennis. And after school hours, tagging round the chain store with them, I had a feeling of watching their 'growing pains' from a long way off—flicking rulers with the College Boys, tussling for each others' scarves. 'We all grew up too soon', I would think, remembering Ginny and the girls in the Home, for I had begun to identify myself with them, and although, technically, I was without the 'experience' of the girls in the Home, the root of their 'experience' lay within my experience, began to stir, on nights like Thursdays, when they began to speak about Friday. For Friday was Pay Day, Dole Day, and Late Night Out.

(Pianist. Sitting-room sounds. Girls singing)

Marta
Rambling Rose of the
Wild wood.
Marta *(etc)*

Peg: Ginny. What's about a swop for Friday? My red for your green net. Every time I put the red on some stumer gets his heel stuck in the underskirt.

Ginny: Change your dance hall then. Try the Dive. Sticking out a mile.

Peg: Not a chance. I know all the crowd at the Red Triangle. But if ye don't want to swop me, you don't need to hedge. Just say it straight out.

Ginny: (Wearily) You can have the green. For I'll not be needing it on Friday. I'm still on the Dole, and you ken fine how Matron feels about Dolers going dancing.

Third Girl: We know. Her face closes up yon wye. And stays closed for a week.

Ginny: (Brightening up) I can tell you this much though. I'm going after a job next week. And if I get a start, I'll be out next Friday. And Matron can just take a running jump.

Peg: Even if you do get a start next week, Ginny, you'll

still no be in pocket. They'll keep a week's lying time off you. I'll tell you what though. If you get a start, me and Maddie will sub you a bob each. *(To Pianist)* Sure we will, Maddie? We'll sub Ginny a bob each. That will see her by on Friday.

Ginny: (To Peg) Ta, hen.

Peg: Roll on next Friday, Ginny. Till you see my new sheik. He's sticking out. Sticking out a mile. Hat. Gloves. The lot. And he speaks pan loaf.

Ginny: Did he see you home last Friday, Peg?

Peg: What do you think? Not on your Nelly. I lost my last fella through taking him right to the door. 'You bide here?' he saud, and he beat it. Scarpered. Homes put some of them off.

Ginny: I know. Once they get the wind you're on probation they either expect everything from you, or they want nothing to do with you at all.

Peg: Do you know what I did though? I kidded this new fella that I lived in one of the houses on the Terrace. You would have died if you saw us, Ginny. Honest, you would. Inside somebody else's lobby. I thought he'd never go, and there was me, my heart in my mouth in case the folk would come out of their own door and show me up.

Narrator: And other days. Days in which they would lean out of the Sitting-room window staring down on the streets which had suckled them. Still drawing a tithe of comfort and revealing a world of resentment.

Ginny: Green ladies! See them pair walking as if they owned the place. I know them. I was brought up in a Home they sent me to.

Mary: What was it like, Ginny?

Ginny: Bloody awful. Do you know what they did, Mary, if you wet your bed? Plumped you right into a cold bath. I beat it though. I beat it off home to my Da again. I could have stayed there, too, but they came to take me back again. My Da nearly lost the head, so he did. But it made no odds.

Mary: I know. I remember—

Narrator: And I did too. For I'd seen it happen so often in the Wynd of my early childhood where they had only their curses or their feet to retaliate with in their conflicts with authority, so that big issues dwindled down into small convictions for assault or Breach of Peace.

Ginny: It made no odds. I'd got to go back to the Home just the same.

Mary: It's no use running away. Even if you get back, you can't stay.

Ginny: Well, you're a fine one to speak, Mary—you're always running away.

Mary: I know, but it's still no use. It's funny, isn't it, Ginny—you ran away from an Orphanage, and I'm always running away to get back to one.

Ginny: But you don't need to run away to go back to the Orphanage. Miss Erskine gives you your fare to go properly.

Mary: I did go properly twice. You remember, Ginny. I borrowed your clothes to go once, but it was no good. You see, Ginny—

Narrator: 'You see, Ginny—' I had wanted so much to make an impression that I wasn't sure which role to adopt, glamorous, sophisticated in Ginny's clothes, or scholarly, in my gym-tunic. But neither role—and I had donned them both—had impressed anyone but the younger children. So that I found another way of easing the awful ache in myself for both the Orphanage and my first remembered home in the Wynd. I would simply set off in the darkness on the road to the countrysides which contained them. There were times when I got near enough to put my hand out and touch the Orphanage walls. My home in the Wynd I never reached; but it was one of my attempts to do so which led to the beginning of the end of my stay in the Girls' Home. It was then too that I discovered that it was not only lack of vocabulary that made my kind inarticulate, for I had words, but none which could be applied to the intangible.

Matron: You wanted to get home. Is that all you can say for yourself and for the anxiety you have caused us all—up in the middle of the night searching the countryside for you. And you wanted to get home. Do you know why you were taken away from your home in the first place?

Mary: Yes.

Matron: You know what kind of life your mother led? Well, did you?

Mary: Yes.

Matron: Were you always aware of it? Or did you learn later?

Mary: I always knew.

Matron: You mean, you saw all that was going on?

Mary: No. No. I just knew.

Matron: Did you think it was wrong?

Mary: It worried me sometimes.

Matron: Why?

Mary: Because I was afraid my mother might like some of the men better than she liked me.

Matron: I see. Despite all that Miss Erskine's done for you, it seems you still lack a moral sense, you want to go back, and you don't think it was wrong. I thought your years in the Orphanage would have ensured that much.

Mary: I didn't say that. I didn't say it wasn't wrong. Just that it never shocked me. And the Orphanage never mentioned it to me in all the years because they knew I wasn't like that.

Narrator: Nor in 'all the years' had Mrs Thane of the Orphanage, incapable by temperament of showing affection, been capable by nature of disliking us on an adult level. It was the first time I had experienced this; for the dislike which had sprung up between myself and the Matron of the Girls' Home at our first meeting was now out in the open, and I didn't know how to cope with it.

(Basement dormitory at night. Door opens)

Ginny: (In bed) Got a dog-end on you, Maddie? Oh, it's you, Mary. Where have you been? It's gone half-past ten.

Peg: (Teasing) She found a 'click' in the flea-pit last night and made a heavy date with him for the night, didn't you, hen?

Mary: No. Matron sent me to Miss Erskine.

Ginny: Not again. What for this time?

Mary: For buying peanuts with my half-crown pocket-money.

Ginny: Don't be daft.

Peg: She's kiddin' us on now. Getting a wise guy in your old age, Mary?

Mary: No. Honestly. Even Miss Erskine laughed, though, when she heard the 'charge'. It was she who gave me the half-crown. She told Matron I could do worse things with it than buy peanuts.

I hate her.

Ginny: Get into your kip, hen, and stop worrying. All that one needs is a night with a good man.

Mary: Ginny. I know she'd be pleased if she ever had anything really bad to report to Miss Erskine. But I'm not going to give her that. I'll kill her first.

Ginny: *(Not really realising)* What with—arsenic?

Mary: *(To self more than to Ginny)* No. I wouldn't do it that way. I'd want her to know that she was dying, and I was doing it. Because she'd know the reason why. She always blames me for her sore heads, but I feel like—

Ginny: Not next week then, hen. I've got no lolly for a wreath. Go to sleep, and hold everything till I catch up on my back-lying board-money.

(Fade)

Narrator: It was after Ginny's back-lying board-money had been repaid. It was the week her Probation Officer had approved of her engagement. And although it was Thursday, normally a dull night in the Home: no money and wash your clothes night, there was a feeling of freedom and privilege that lent vicarious gaiety to everyone in the sitting-room.

(Maddie, Pianist, and girls)

Oh, oh Antonio
He's gone away
Left me alon-i-o
All on my own-i-o
I would like to see him with
His ice cream cart
But off you go, Antonio
And you're my sweet-heart.

Peg: Right enough, Ginny, the Probation Officer's not a bad stick when it gets down to brass tacks.

Maddie: This time next week you'll be living it up at the party.

Ginny: What about having a barney on our own? To get a bit of practice in. And we could start by doing something about your clock, Peg; you just never make the best of yourself.

Maddie: She wants to get rid o' that frizz for a start.

Peg: What do you mean, frizz! It's me new perm. I only got it done last Friday.

Ginny: It's all gone to frizz since last Friday. I'm going to set it for you, so that the new style can settle down before next week.

(Fade in Pianist and girls singing)

Antonio . . .

Ginny: (In midst of running commentary as she 'restyles' Peg) What you want, Peg, is a wee touch of sun-tan powder to cover thae pimples and a bit of my Autumn Berry lipstick to give you a touch of colour.

Narrator: If only I could paint. The desire struck me as I sat watching Ginny. 'I'd paint Ginny. She's so vivid. If only I could paint.'

Ginny: Yes. You, Mary! Your turn next. Dreamy Danny.

Peg: I'm dying to see what Mary would really look like out of that gym-tunic and proper made-up.

Maddie: She can have the loan of my black flared and . . .

Ginny: Press your lips together, Mary, to set the lipstick. Don't lick it, stumer! You'll get a second coat on in a minute.

Peg: (Near, hovering over Mary. Acting it in fun—a mimicry of Charles Boyer) Darleenk. I love you so veree much. This love I have for you, it is keeling me.

Ginny: Cut it out, Peg. Stop acting the goat. And don't you dare move, Mary, till I come back with the mirror.

Narrator: Cinderella. Ready for the ball. Staring at myself. Not knowing whether I liked myself or not, but intrigued by the difference.

(Girls; genuinely enthusiastic, whether about their own handiwork or their model hard to say)

Ginny: She's stickin' out—

Peg: Stickin' out a mile! *(Great compliment)*

Maddie: She could easily get a fella when she's proper dressed and made-up.

Ginny: You want to go dancing, Mary. You want to learn. All the sheiks are in the dance halls. It's easy. Come on. I'll lead. You've only got to follow.

(Pianist, others singing: 'Blaze Away'—quickstep)

We'll make a bonfire of our troubles,
Then we'll watch them blaze away,
And when they all go up in smoke-clouds . . .

Ginny: Relax . . . Quick, Quick, Turn. Let yourself go, Mary.

(Piano, singers)

And as the bonfire keeps on burning

Happy days will be returning
For while the band keeps playing . . .

Ginny: (Exhausted by laughter and efforts to teach Mary) Let's have a polka. She doesn't glide; she jumps. Come on, Mary. Once more. *(Much laughter)*

(Pianist and girls singing accompaniment to dancers)

You should see me dance the Polka
You should see me turn it round,
You should see me dance the Polka
While my petticoats hit the ground.

(Much laughter)

Matron: What is the meaning of all this noise? Mary! What is the reason for this ridiculous get-up?

Ginny: We dressed Mary up for a tear—Doesn't she look different all made-up?

Matron: Yes. Yes. She looks the part all right.

Narrator: This was the one time that the Matron was too slow to put the door between herself and the usual quiet, last-minute barbs from her tongue. For I reached the door first. I remember shaking her by the shoulders till all the coward she was appealed in fear out of her eyes. I remember thinking as I shook, 'Now, you really have got something to report me for this time.' And it didn't matter. Not even when Ginny came down to the dormitory to tell me—

Ginny: You've done it this time, Mary. She really is ill. They've sent for the doctor and the Committee and Miss Erskine. And you're just sitting there on the bed not even looking sorry.

Mary: I'm not, Ginny. I'm not sorry. Never sorry.

(Fade)

Narrator: Never sorry. Not even when it meant a transfer to a Home for Difficult Girls and finally admission to a Mental Hospital—the only solution my guardian could now find.

Miss Erskine: I no longer know what to do with you, Mary. None of the Homes will have you back again. No one can be expected to put up with this running away. If only I knew what it is you want, what it is that you are running away from—or to?

Mary: I want to go back. Home, to the Wynd and to the Orphanage.

Miss Erskine: But I always allowed you to go back and see them all at the Orphanage. You never needed to run away to get there.

Mary: I know. It's not that kind of back. I mean—it's just—

Miss Erskine: It's just—What, Mary? What is it just?

Mary: It's just I don't feel about things and people any more. Not the way I used to feel about them when I was in the Wynd and in the Orphanage. I used to be terribly excited and happy, and looking forward. I haven't been like that since I left.

Miss Erskine: But nobody can expect to feel about people and things as they did in childhood. That they don't is just one of the signs of growing up. And you are growing up now, you know, Mary.

Mary: But I'd rather never grow up than stop feeling and caring. I wouldn't mind if I died now, because I don't think anything will happen to me again that matters.

Miss Erskine: What did matter then, Mary?

Mary: Just everything.

Miss Erskine: But what kind of thing?

Mary: (More to self) My dominie, Mrs Thane. It mattered so much when they were pleased with what you did. And just as much when they weren't. And my desk and my bed and my locker, and summer, and winter. They all mattered.

Miss Erskine: I think, you know, Mary, what you really need is a rest, a real rest, away from everything for a while.

(Fade out)

II

Narrator: Do not expect again a Phoenix hour
Sudden the rain of gold
And heart's first ease.

(Fade up ward sounds. Old patient singing 'Bonnie Gallowa'')

Narrator: In that 'while' or 'rest' which was to stretch into a year, it was the night of my admission to the Mental Hospital which remains static and still unreal in memory. For, though I had signed myself in as a patient, I did not then know that I couldn't sign myself out again; nor had I quite realised just exactly what being a patient meant, till I lay in the ward, with that smell of stale biscuits which I ever afterwards was to associate with paraldehyde, drifting round me.

(Fade up ward sounds and 'Bonnie Gallowa'')

First Patient: (Next bed to Mary Carron) What are they going to do to you?

Mary: I don't know.

First Patient: They're going to hang me . . . from a high hill top.

Mary: (As to herself) . . . from a high hill top.

(Fade up ward sounds and 'Bonnie Gallowa'')

Mary: (Savouring words to self) from a high hill top; from a high hill top.

First Nurse: (Fairly distant) That's enough now, Bonnie Gallowa'. That's enough for another night. Time for your bed.

Mary: From a high hill top
From a high hill top . . .

Old Ellen: It's that coarse, coarse man o' mine again, Nurse. Nab, nab, nabbin' at my poor ears. Nobody knows. Nobody . . .

Mary: (Losing herself in her rhyme again)
From a high hill top
From a high hill top.
They're hanging me tomorrow *(Louder)*
From a high hill top.

First Nurse: (Near: sudden) You're having a nice little chat with yourself, are you then, Mary? That's fine. *(Going away)* But it's time to sleep now. So just you settle down.

(Fade in ward noises. 'Bonnie Gallowa'')

Old Ellen: That coarse, coarse man o' mine, Nursie. Nab, nab, nabbin' awa at my poor ears.

First Nurse: Don't you mind him, Ellen. Come on, let's get you into your bed.

Mary: (Suddenly—fairly loudly) Nurse! Nurse!

First Nurse: What is it, Mary?

Mary: Nurse, I don't really speak to myself. I never speak to myself.

First Nurse: Of course you don't. Nobody speaks to themselves in here. Just you try to get some sleep now. *(Going off)* Lindley! Get Bonnie Gallowa' and Ellen into bed now, before Nurse Fraser comes on.

Mary: *(As to self)* I'll tell her tomorrow when it's all quiet. I'll tell her tomorrow that I don't speak to myself. She'll believe me then. *(Rhyme comes back to her rescue in that she loses awareness of things in it. Very quietly to herself)*

From a high hill top
From a high hill top . . .

Narrator: It was when the Charge Nurse of the ward came in that I knew I would never have to explain to anyone that I didn't really speak to myself.

C N Fraser: *(Approaching Nurse)* How's everything in here, Nurse?

1st Nurse: Fine, Nurse Fraser. There's an admission.

C N Fraser: A re-admission?

First Nurse: No. New. Acute neurasthenia. Here's the admission form.

C N Fraser: Mary Carron. The Orphanage, Skene. Mary Carron. The Orphanage. *(Slight Fade)*

First Nurse: Mary! Mary Carron. Here's someone to see you.

C N Fraser: Hullo. Hullo Mary. Do you remember me?

Mary: Yes, I remember you fine. You're Margaret Fraser.

C N Fraser: That's right.

Mary: You was the maid at the Orphanage when I first came there.

C N Fraser: And that's some years ago.

Mary: You sat on the dresser and mended the sheets and you baked the scones, and made the pease-brose and bathed me on Saturdays—till a new maid came.

C N Fraser: That's right, too. Isn't this a fine thing to have happened to you, Mary?

Mary: I'm not mad, or anything like that. I'm just here for three months for a rest.

C N Fraser: Well, get down in your bed then and try to get some rest. Goodnight, Mary.

Narrator: It was with the passing of the days that I realised that my relationship with Charge Nurse Fraser was both bond and barrier. For the country which had contained the Orphanage and reared us both, had also conditioned our natures into a reserve which was rarely broken.

Yet I was always conscious of her presence in the ward and immediately aware of her absence. Awaiting her return on her day off, a thousand questions tripping on my tongue. The school. The Kirk. Berryhill, and Loch of Skene. But it was my eyes which searched her face for an answer to the true urgencies. My dominie. Mrs Thane. Nana, my school friend. Did you see all of them? Or even any one of them? And did they speak of me? And failing to find the answer in her face, I would return to my corner beside the ward window, to continue the endless letters I wrote to them in my mind, without a beginning and without an ending.

Mary: (Fade up) Truly I didn't. I didn't do any of the kind of things you would think bad: lying, stealing, swearing. It was just—I was unhappy. I missed you all. I couldn't settle down in any place, or to anything.

Narrator: Letters of the mind which, through time, became spasmodic, addressed to nobody in particular and condensed to four words: forgive me; I'm sorry. Time, at first unnoticed, became marked off by the daily walk round the grounds.

(Ward noises and radio: singer singing 'Easter Parade')

In your Easter bonnet
With all the frills upon it,
You'll be the grandest lady
In the Easter Parade.
I'll be all in clover
And when they look you over—

First Nurse: Walk. Ladies. Hats and coats now. Jump to it, Mary. See that Ellen doesn't go burying herself in a hat that's too big for her.

Ellen: It's that man of mine again, Mary. Coarse, coarse man. Nab, nabbin' away at my poor ears.

Mary: Never mind that man, Ellen. Keep your head still a wee minute till I sort your hat. You could be anybody now, Ellen. You could—

Second Nurse: Get moving, Mary. Take Ellen's arm, now.

Narrator: And Ellen could have been anybody, or almost anybody. Standing quietly waiting for her arm to be taken, her hat straight on her head. 'I'd speak to Ellen,' I thought. 'I'd speak to her if I passed her on a country road. I'd say "It's a fine day", because looking at her now you wouldn't know . . .'

(Outside sounds)

First Nurse: Hurry, Ladies. Keep moving now.

(Workman whistling tune of 'In your Easter Bonnet')

Narrator: I heard the workman whistling before I saw him.

It was the first time I had seen anyone from what had now become to my mind 'the outside', and I had a sudden impulse to break away from the crocodile and rush up and say: I'm not mad. Truly I'm not. I'm as sane as you. Help me. *(Workman whistling)*

Narrator: But he wouldn't believe me. I knew he wouldn't.

First Nurse: (Distant) What's holding us up now? Your shoe again, Annie?

Second Nurse: (In reply) No. It's Mary this time. You're standing there in a dwam, Mary. Holding up the line. Get a move on now.

Mary: (Starts to laugh, quietly at first, then uncontrollably)

First Nurse: (To Second Nurse) What on earth's come over her?

Second Nurse: She's surely a bit on the hilarious side, this morning.

Mary: (Suddenly stops laughing) I'm not hilarious, Nurse. It isn't that. Truly it isn't. It's just the song the man was whistling.

In your Easter bonnet . . .
You'll be the grandest lady . . .

And here's me—in this big hat. It's so big that if the sun was shining I wouldn't have a shadow.

First Nurse: What do you mean, you wouldn't have a shadow?

Second Nurse: And what's more the sun isn't shining, so you don't have to worry then. Do you?

Mary: No. Nurse! Nurse!

Second Nurse: (Fairly distant) What is it now, Mary?

Mary: (Near) Nothing. Just—Nurse, we always used to laugh at funny hats when I was outside.

Narrator: I was no longer 'outside' and I tried to fall back on my old childhood ability of shutting out the panics that sometimes seized my spirit, by bringing the full force of my concentration down on small, inanimate things that didn't matter. It was when this ability proved no longer foolproof that I discovered another, when only the tip of my nose jutted out under my wide hat into that microscopic spring.

First Nurse: (Shouting to Nurses at back end of crocodile) Hurry up, Ladies. Just once more round the new block. We want to get back before the rain comes.

Second Nurse: (In conversation with First) When is the Chief due in our Ward anyhow?

First Nurse: Elevenish. But you never know with the Chief. He sometimes makes it sooner.

Old Ellen: . . . Coarse. Coarse man of mine, Mary. He's at it again. Nab. Nab, nabbin' at my poor ears.

Second Nurse: Take Ellen's arm now, Mary. Don't let her lag behind this morning. We want to get back to the Ward on time.

First Nurse: (Looking at watch) And we won't if we don't get a move on.

Second Nurse: Doesn't time fly, just? It doesn't seem like three months since the Chief's last round.

First Nurse: Did Fraser give you any inkling of who's to be sent down to Ward X this time?

Come on now, Ladies. Move a bit quicker.

Mary: (As to self) Ward X . . . Ward X . . . Ward . . .

Old Ellen: Nobody knows. Nobody. Nab. Nab. Nabbin' . . .

Second Nurse: Mary! Didn't I tell you to take Ellen's arm?

Mary: Put your hand inside my pocket, Ellen. *(As to self)*

Ward X—the Forever Place. Don't let it be me. Ward X—don't let—Don't let . . . *(To Ellen)* It's warmer with both our hands inside my pocket, isn't it, Ellen?

Old Ellen: Nobody knows, Mary. That man—coarse, coarse man. Nobody—Nab, nab, nabbin'. Nobody knows.

Mary: (As to self) It might be me. Don't . . . don't let me be sent down to Ward X . . . A damsel with a dulcimer. Don't let me . . .

In a vision once I saw
It was an Abyssinian maid
Singing of Mount Abora—

First Nurse: (Sudden, near) . . . her other glove, Mary. Ellen's other glove. Did you see it?

Mary: Yes. It's here, in my pocket.

First Nurse: Well then. Why didn't you say so in the first place? I've been asking you for the last five minutes.

Second Nurse: She's always the same, that Mary Carron—miles away.

First Nurse: Inside now, Ladies, quickly! The Chief's just come out of the new block. He'll be round in the ward in a minute. *(Fade)*

Narrator: . . . Could I revive within me her symphony and song . . . I said my poems the way that children count to themselves to ward off evil moments and speed the good ones. But the verse was never composed which could out-time the duration of the Chief's Quarterly Round. For then it was that the patients for whom there was little hope of recovery were transferred to Ward X, that Forever Place.

(Ward noises, 'Bonnie Gallowa' ', Ellen)

Mary: (As to self) That with music loud and long, I would build . . .

Chief: (Approaching) Good morning, Nurse.

C N Fraser: Good morning, sir.

Chief: Now, let us see—

Mary: (To self) That sunny dome . . .

Chief: And Ellen?

Mary: Those caves of ice.

C N Fraser: Little change, sir. Lucid only now and then.

Mary: And all who saw
Would cry beware . . .

Chief: How is Miss Mavor responding?

C N Fraser: Slowly; her response is very slight.

Chief: . . . And Mary Carron? *(Near to Mary)* Good morning, Mary.

Mary: (To self, furiously fast) Where Alph the sacred river ran through caverns measureless to man, down to a sunless sea where twice five miles—where twive . . . five niles . . . Don't let me . . .

C N Fraser: (Near, sudden) That's it then, Lindley. Here are the charts of the Ladies who are going down to Ward X: Beattie, Miss Mavor and Sarah.

First Nurse: Is this the lot?

C N Fraser: That's the lot.

Narrator: It was only then that my face felt free of the pressure of the Chief's face staring down on it; and then that sweat ran down me and then that words had width, confined to none; embracing all. Thank you. Oh, thank you.

For another three months had passed, and I had again escaped that Forever Place, Ward X. I think now, of each period of three months spent in the Mental Hospital, as a kind of canopy in time, under which I hid, safe and unsafe, like all hiding places. No longer was I distressed by my fellow-patients' hallucinations as reality, lest the nurses would think I shared them. It was no longer 'inside' that disrupted me, but echoes from the 'outside'; like visiting days. I seldom had a visitor. Yet, on such days, the telephone never rang but my heart leapt up to answer to it. Please, ring for me next time. Let your very next ring be a visitor for me. In times like these it was Charge Nurse Fraser who broke the apprehension of my listening vigil.

C N Fraser: (Approaching) Mary. *(Near)* Come on! You and me have places to go. Get your coat. We'll go down to the shop in the grounds and have our tea together.

Mary: But I can't. Maybe . . . Maybe the telephone . . .

C N Fraser: No maybe about it. The visitors will all be leaving in a minute; we want to get there before the rush starts. Now! What shall we have for our tea? *(Fade)*

Narrator: It was when the telephone did work the magic with which I bequeathed it—that even the ward seemed taken by my own surprise.

C N Fraser: Lindley! Take Mary's visitor round from the front. *(To Mary)* Yes. It is for you. You've been listening long enough for it. So come on. A clean apron for you, my girl.

(Door opens and closes)

Mary: Hullo. Hullo, Ginny. You got my letter then? How are you, Ginny?

Ginny: Mary! Your hair. It's cut to your ears. It will never take a perm.

Mary: Sit down, Ginny.

Ginny: We'll no be locked in here, will we?

Mary: No. You can sit down on my bed, Ginny.

Ginny: Is that the get-up you all wear in here? It's terrible, so it is. And it's no funny.

Mary: I know. It wasn't that I was laughing at, Ginny. It's you, your face. I forget how I look, you see. But I must look terrible, by your face. I've got a frock; a lovely frock. My guardian gave it to me when she last came to see me.

Ginny: Will they no let you wear it in here then?

Mary: They wouldn't mind. I could wear it if I wanted to. It's just—I don't need a frock.

Ginny: And your stockings, Mary! They're like men's pink woollen combinations, by God.

Narrator: 'They only reach my knees,' I thought. 'And my legs are bare till they reach my knickers, and they're navy-blue. Thank goodness Ginny doesn't know that, or that I feel just like a small red scrubbed girl under my long flannel frock.'

Mary: Ginny, tell me something.

Ginny: What?

Mary: Everything, Ginny. When you got my letter did you—

Ginny: Is this where you sleep, hen?

Mary: Yes. I got this room all to myself to sleep in last week. Before that I slept in the ward with all the women.

Ginny: But there's no bars on your window, Mary. You could scarper if you wanted. You could easily scarper.

Mary: Where—out of that window?

Ginny: Sure. That's how I beat it from the Home when I was a kid.

Mary: Try that window.

(Ginny does so)

Ginny: I can't shove it up any further than this.

Mary: Neither can I, Ginny.

Ginny: Do they lock this door? *(Examining)* No they can't. There's no knob on it or anything.

Mary: The knob's on the other side.

Ginny: But how do you get out?

Mary: I don't. Not till a Nurse unlocks it in the morning. Do you know something, Ginny, if ever I get out of here, I think I'll stay surprised when a door opens just because I turn its knob.

Ginny: If I was locked up in here all night, I'd wreck the place. Honest to God I would.

Mary: No you wouldn't, Ginny. Not if you wanted to get out. You'd feel like that. I do sometimes; especially when I hear the key turning the last thing at night. I want to beat the door down with my hands, and scream my head off because you feel so shut away. So forgotten. Ginny. Tell me. When you got my letter was you surprised to see that I was in here?

Ginny: In a way, yes. In a way, no. You always was a bit queer. Different from the rest of us. But we never thought you was soft in the head; not asylum mad, if you savvy. You have changed though, Mary. You look terribly different.

Narrator: And yet, Ginny had to seek for the 'difference'. I felt her searching my face for some trace of it, like 'outside' people did. 'She's expecting me to be mad,' I thought. 'Even Ginny.'

Ginny: Well then, do you know, Mary?

Mary: Know what?

Ginny: Know when you're going to get out of here?

Mary: No.

Ginny: But you could ask. The doctor would know. He could tell you when.

Mary: That's why I've never asked. He might tell me the truth, Ginny. He might say 'Never'. And I'd rather not know that.

(Fade out)

Narrator: For the time was still to come when I was to know just how the spirit would react when hope was almost gone. It was on a day when a lady came to see me out of visiting hours. Her proposition was unexpected and entrancing.

Lady: . . . And that is where your typing would come in useful, Mary. This doctor needs some help. In return you would have pocket-money; all the books you can read and freedom of a lovely countryside—Larbert—it's in Perthshire. I want you to think it over.

Mary: But it doesn't need thinking over. Of course I'll go. I'm ready to go tomorrow.

Lady: No, not quite as quick as all that. Take a day or two to think it over and I'll be back to see how you decide. *(Fade out)*

Mary: But, Nurse Fraser, imagine! The hills of Perthshire. Books, pocket-money, my own clothes. I don't need even two minutes to think it over. I'm going. I'm going to go.

C N Fraser: Now, look Mary. Calm yourself, and begin from the beginning. What exactly did the lady tell you?

Mary: She said I could get out of here. I could do some

typing and things for a doctor. It's in a place called Larbert in Perthshire. It's a lovely place, she says, Nurse Fraser. And do you know—

C N Fraser: (Calling passing nurse) Lindley! Will you give out the draughts for me? Catch. Here's the keys. *(To Mary)* Mary, come here for a minute, will you? *(Near)* Shut the door behind you.

(Door shut) Do you know about Larbert, Mary?

Mary: I know the countryside is lovely.

C N Fraser: And you won't see much of it. For Larbert also has the biggest Mental Hospital in Scotland. Did you know that?

Mary: No, Nurse Fraser.

C N Fraser: You see, you might never get out of here, Mary, that I don't know. But what I do know is this: here at least you know where you are and the people you are with. It's up to you, of course, Mary, but if I were you, when the lady comes back for an answer, I'd say no.

Narrator: 'You may never get out of here'. It was the 'never' that my spirit fixed upon, and looking back, strangely enough, that was the easier interpretation to accept. For 'never', which cancelled today and obliterated tomorrow, freed me completely of my former instinct to submerge my natural emotions. I could laugh now without fear of being thought 'hilarious', and withdraw into my corner by the ward-window and into myself without fear of being considered 'depressed'. Old Ellen's 'coarse, coarse man' who haunted all our Ground Walks together, began to have more reality for me, than the sudden recollections which forced themselves up out of the far-away normality of her former country days; 'Oh, Mary, the cheese and milk and fine sweet crowdie'—leaving me without words. A damnable, unpredictable thing was memory, even when you tried to press it down and confine it into one day. 'It's Friday again because there's fish for dinner and plum duff.' Lying deep and unexpected, memory could suddenly explode, hurtling deceptions of itself aside, and leaving you vulnerable and 'first time', as on my second Christmas in the Hospital.

(Ward sounds. Nurses singing carols. 'Child in a Manger' in Gaelic. Ward noises)

First Nurse: (As in passing) It's time you were getting ready now, Mary. Your name's down for the Patients' Christmas Dance.

Mary: I don't want to go, Nurse. Not looking like this.

First Nurse: But you're not going looking like that; you're putting on that new dress your guardian gave you. I wouldn't mind being you tonight, Mary. You can only dance with the male attendants, and I can only dance with the male patients. So I know who I'd be tonight. Come on, now, into the bathroom and I'll help you to get dressed up. *(Fade)* Shoes, now. What about shoes? You can't wear your heavy ground shoes. What size do you take, Mary? I mean, what size did you take 'outside'?

Mary: I took four and a half outside.

First Nurse: Well, mine are size five and a half, but anyhow, we can try them. Your feet will probably have grown a bit in a year. How's that? Do they fit all right?

Mary: They're fine. They just fit me fine, Nurse.

First Nurse: Well, that's that settled. I told you your feet would have grown a bit in a year. Some face powder now. Here you are! Well, go on. Use it. Did you not use powder outside, Mary?

Mary: (As to self) A year. It's a whole year now. *(To nurse)* It's a year, Nurse. A whole year!

First Nurse: Look, let me powder your face for you. The stuff's all over you.

Mary: But Nurse, it's a year now.

First Nurse: Now! That's it. That's better. A little lipstick and you'll be all set. Keep still, Mary, or you'll have it all over your chin. Now, look at yourself. Isn't that different? *(Goes to door and calls)* Lindley, Nurse Lindley. Here a minute. *(Near)* Doesn't Mary look different now?

Second Nurse: We're not going to have a look-in at the dance tonight once you step in, Mary.

First Nurse: That's just what I said. She's going to get her pick of all the attendants. Stop it, now, Mary. Stop crying. You're going to spoil all your new face.

Second Nurse: I'm beginning to think you are daft, Mary. I've never seen you crying before and here you are crying about a happy thing like looking bonny.

First Nurse: That's it. That's better. No wonder you're laughing at yourself now, you daft ha'pence. Here, let me powder your nose again.

Mary: Nurse, thank you for the shoes. I'll give you them back tomorrow.

First Nurse: That's all right. You hold on to them. You can wear them when you get out of here.

Narrator: 'When you get out of here.' Although it was a Junior Nurse who said that, it was the first time anyone official had mentioned my going out, and not just as a possibility, but simply as a matter of fact.

(Dance Band—'Ye Banks and Braes' into 'Rowan Tree' into 'Cock of the North')

It seems to me now that my second spring in the Mental Hospital outblossomed all other springs. But that, of course, is true only in retrospect, and only because of the suddenness with which I was thrust out into it, so that memory stands still in a spring which seems as large and white and enamelled as it had seemed in childhood. I was setting the bed-patients' trays for lunch in the concentrated, privilege-conscious way I did all the small jobs which had now become exclusively mine. I was remembering not to give knives and forks to suicidal patients and I was thinking, 'I know who the suicidal patients are. I'm trusted to know. Just as I am trusted to make the nurses' toast in the morning, in the pantry, with the long fork. Only I've got to hide the fork and fly if I hear any of the matrons and doctors coming, because I'm not supposed to be away on my own'. If it wouldn't get the nurses into trouble I'd like fine if the doctor was to catch me sitting away toasting the bread in the pantry, because then he'd know the nurses think I'm well. Some day maybe—some day I'll pretend I didn't hear the doctor coming and he'll catch me and he'll know for himself then.

(Ward noises. Telephone ringing)

Mary: That's your tray, Annie.

Old Annie: That damned craitturs, Mary, all over my bed. Beetles. Not a minute's peace. You'll kill them for me, Mary.

Mary: In a minute. When I've given Miss Henry her tray. In a minute, Annie.

Old Annie: Damned beetles. Damned craitturs all over my bed.

C N Fraser: Mary. Come here. Never mind the trays. Just put them down and come into the bathroom.

Mary: But it isn't bath day, Nurse Fraser. I was bathed yesterday.

Narrator: Maybe, I thought to myself as I stood in the middle of the dinner-time ward with the trays in my hand, maybe, I'm going to get a bath all by myself after this, and none of the old women will see me naked any more. Maybe Nurse Fraser's going to give me another privilege.

C N Fraser: It's your bath day! So come on, Mary. Don't stand there wondering about it. Give Nurse Lindley your trays now, and hurry up.

Narrator: It was when I got into the bathroom that I saw all my own clothes lying folded on the chair. Even so, I still couldn't take in what Nurse Fraser was telling me.

C N Fraser: I knew yesterday, I knew you were getting out today, but I didn't tell you because it would have sent you right up to High Doh and that might have finished that. I thought this was safest.

Mary: But I can't be getting out, Nurse Fraser. I've got nobody to take me out.

C N Fraser: Your Domicile, the parish of your birth, is taking you out. High time, too, for I've enough on my hands without you. Now, listen. Mary, listen carefully. For the next three months you're going to stay with an old woman in a croft up in the Highlands. If you stick that out for three months you'll never be back here again.

Mary: I'm never going to come back here.

C N Fraser: We don't think you will, that's why you're getting out. But, remember Mary, remember this: stick it. It can't be harder than here. Do you remember Inverness-shire and the Highlands at all, Mary?

Mary: No.

Narrator: No. And I didn't remember. I could only remember as far back as the Wynd, the Orphanage, the Girls' Home, and none of them had been my Domicile—my place.

(Slight fade)

C N Fraser: There's all the best of the spring in front of you yet. It's lovely up there in the Highlands in the spring. I remember one holiday—

Narrator: Domicile. My place. The word was new to me, and like all new words as lovely in its strangeness as in its interpretation as in its sound—place of birth. Maybe, maybe that which lay at the beginning of everything lay at the end of it, too, like a circle; so that you could go round and round, never really knowing where the circle began or where it ended.

C N Fraser: You'll have to say goodbye to Old Ellen and Annie, Mary. You can't go without saying goodbye to them. They're going to miss you.

Narrator: And I was going to miss them too. I knew that. I knew it just as I knew that I couldn't go without saying goodbye to them even though they couldn't understand. And maybe it was because they didn't realise it was goodbye that I cried for the second and last time in the Mental Hospital.

C N Fraser: And I don't suppose you've got a hankie. *(Shouts)* Lindley! Nurse Lindley, bring some hankies for Mary, will you? *(Nearer)* No! A hankie's no good. Bring a sheet instead. This daft lassie's crying here because we're letting her out.

(Fade crying)

PART VI

MOMENT OF COMMUNICATION

MOMENT OF COMMUNICATION WITH A LIST D GIRL

F*** Off!
She said.
Dismissing me
and my persuasions
with a contemptuous stare
that crinkled to a smile
of small surprise
when I
in anger roared—
F*** Off
to Where??

PART VII

SINGLE JOURNEY

SINGLE JOURNEY

'I WILL be coming on the *Flying Scotsman.* Monday first. It gets into Waverley round about three o'clock.'

Two days, and five hours travelling time away, and she would be Home. Or nearly. For she had cheated about home, these past years in London.

'I come from Edinburgh,' she had always said to people who traced her Scottish accent. Everybody had heard of Edinburgh, but nobody in London would ever have heard of the small village of Trapmain, lying under the Law. Except, perhaps, exiles like herself.

'I'll miss Covent Garden,' she wrote. 'And Sandra and Babs.' And that was true, she thought, rising to stare down on the now deserted Market. She had never walked through Covent Garden on her way to the Office in the morning, without a sudden rising of spirit; the shrill, appreciative wolf whistles of the Porters, their quick Cockney badinage: 'Mind how you go, Miss! Old Sid ain't so old! Not when he gets down to unloading them there Passion Fruits!' The sharp, wet tang of chrysanthemums that marked the coming of Autumn on the calendar of the mind, and the first frail daffodils that foretold the Spring.

'But of course,' she wrote, 'with Covent Garden soon to be demolished, and our flat to come under the bulldozers as well, there was no point in staying on . . .'

'You'll sign, Chris!' Sandra had urged, thrusting the Petition to Save Covent Garden under her nose. 'All the Tenants' Association are signing. Not that it will save the Garden, but just,' Sandra had put on her pleading smile, 'just for Old Sakes' Sake!'

And she had signed, remembering as she did so, something she had once read somewhere; 'The only worthwhile Causes are the Lost Causes'. Strange, how you could know something for years, without knowing its true meaning.

'But why you, Sandra?' she had asked. 'Why do you bother? You're leaving to get married! Away to settle down in Sunny Sussex!'

'I told you!' Sandra had reminded her, still smiling. 'For Sakes' Sake! Besides,' she had accused, 'you're leaving yourself! Back to Bonnie Scotland. Promoted. And all that.'

'I could, I suppose,' she wrote, 'have found a flat elsewhere, and stayed on in London, but when the Firm decided to open an office in Edinburgh, and offered me a transfer and an increase in salary because I knew their system, it seemed the sensible thing to do, with Sandra and Babs both leaving to get married, and the flat under sentence of demolition.'

But then, she recalled, she had always done the sensible thing. Only three years older than both Sandra and Babs, she had often felt like their maiden aunt. The one who saved the 5p's for the bath meter; collected the shares of the rent. And delivered it on time! Paid the milkman. Took the clothes to the cleaners, and kept the tickets in a safe place. But, most important of all, kept the stock-pot going with marrow bones and vegetables from Covent Garden, in the lean, last days before the salary cheques came.

'Dear positive girl!' Sandra would say, sniffing appreciatively tound the kitchen. 'We'd die of starvation before the twenty-eighth, if we hadn't got you!'

Maybe that was it. Maybe she had been too 'positive'. Positive about going to London, when Alan had wanted her to stay. 'We could manage, Chris,' he had urged. 'Other couples do! I've got a grant. Not very much, I know. But I could always take a night job. And you've got a good job.'

'You've got a good job, too!' She could still recall the bitterness in her voice. 'A good job. One with prospects. Assistant Sales Manager. We could get married on that salary. Now you suddenly want to chuck it up. And become a student again!'

'You don't understand, Chris—'

And she hadn't understood. Three years at Moray House, studying for a Diploma in Social Work. Three years on a grant of eight pounds a week!

'I want to do something more than spend my life drumming up sales of Ball Bearings and Component Parts', Alan had tried to explain. 'I want to work with people, and for people.'

'But I am people too, Alan.' Her heart protested at the memory. 'We are people. And I need you. As I thought you needed me.'

Maybe, if her heart had spoken for her at the time, it might have helped, might at least have chipped at the wall of misunderstanding that had risen up between them. Maybe . . .

Maybe not, though. She had come to realise over the years in London, that what she and Alan had had was companionship, getting on well together in the daily routine of the Office, sharing its problems, sharing their leisure hours, long Sunday tramps across the Braids, or along the sands at Aberlady. Taking each other comfortably for granted. We get along together as well as most people, we'll get married some day. No rose in the heart.

And of course, it wasn't enough. You could tell when it was enough in other people! She had recognised it immediately, on the night that Sandra had come flying into the Flat, grabbing Chris to herself, and whirling her round the small sitting-room to the ridiculous words of the latest Pop number.

Don't you KNOW
He said HULLO
to ME!

'Oh, Chris! He's noticed me! He's noticed me at last!'

Don't you KNOW
He said HULLO
to ME!

'I could have arrived before the weekend,' she wrote. 'But I promised Sandra that I would be her bridesmaid.

And I see from your letter that you've got to be in Edinburgh on Monday morning anyhow.'

'That suits me fine,' her mother had written. 'I can easily meet your train, as I've got an appointment with the optician, first thing Monday morning.

'I was speaking to Alan Badenoch's mother, the other day. She was telling me that he has just graduated. He goes to London next week, to work at some place called Phoenix House. Apparently they look after young people who take drugs. It seemed strange to think that he is going away to London, just as you are coming home from it . . .'

'I'm sorry to be losing you,' the landlady said, when Chris handed her the keys of the flat. You were a nice crowd of girls. But then we'll all soon have to leave Covent Garden. And of course, you're going Home. No place like it! Is there, now, dear?'

No matter how much the men swept the Garden, the cabbage leaves always seemed to elude them, Chris remembered, as she scuffed her way through them. When the New Market was built, they said it would be completely covered in. A pity, she thought, as she turned into Drury Lane. A pity never to scuff your feet through the wayward cabbage leaves again.

PART VIII

THE USELESS ONE

THE USELESS ONE:

CHRONICLE OF FAILURE

'SHE should,' my publishers had written in their introduction, 'be in the forefront of British Literature.' Me they were speaking about! Mind you, I myself sometimes felt that. But self praise, as they say, is no honour. And when my mood of euphoria had passed, and I thought about it, I realised that success and failure are relative things. As Professor Joad used to say, it all depends what you mean . . . !

The Orphanage Trustees had the final word. No University Education. That was explicit in the letter the dominie had enclosed with my Higher Leaving Certificate: 'My efforts were unavailing. But, you have the gift. You never know what the years will bring to you yet. But *festina lente, festina lente.*' It was no good asking the Matron what the phrase meant. She wouldn't know either! But I knew that it meant something important. For the dominie had never uttered an unimportant word!

'I tried to prepare you for this,' Matron said, vindicating herself, as she folded my aprons for Kitchen Work on a farm. 'But you would set your mind on it!' The last thing to go into my tin trunk was the Bible the Minister had given me in the lugubrious hope that 'God's Grace' would go with me. I wept then. Surprising myself and embarrassing the Minister by my sudden onrush of tears. I, who had only once wept, in all my years at the Orphanage. The reason for my tears eluded me. Whether of joy for escaping from the Orphanage, or of regret for leaving what had become familiar.

'And of course,' Matron had rattled her keys, and waddled across to her desk, 'we must not forget these!' I, certainly had never forgotten them, I thought, as Matron withdrew the bundle of letters from her desk . . .

. . . Friday! Band of Hope night. And a penny for always remembering the Pledge:

I promise here by Grace Divine
To take no Spirits, Ale or Wine:
Nor will I buy nor sell nor give
Strong drink to others while I live.

And a boy with a quiff in his hair, grasping my hand and racing Orphanage-wards with me in the dusk. His 'Friday letter' with crosses for kisses tucked inside my coat pocket.

The agony of keeping a weather eye on Fridays, from the moment they dawned. All childhood's spells invoked, to keep away the rain that would prevent me from getting to the Band of Hope:

Rainie Rainie Rattlestanes
Dinna rain on me
Rain on Johnnie Groat's house
Far across the sea.

Not that the younger girls cared one way or another. They could never remember the Pledge. Either that, or they had made up their minds to drink themselves to death the moment they left the Orphanage. And they had not yet attracted a boy with a quiff in his hair.

'Matron,' Chris informed me, in the important voice we always used when prophesying each other's doom, 'wants to see you in her sitting-room at once!'

'It's for something bad,' I accepted the inevitable with stoicism. 'Little Children Love Ye One Another,' the text on the dining-room wall had always exhorted us. But we had never loved one another. The need for self-preservation had always been so fierce. Even if we had suddenly been blessed with Parents, we would have flung them all under a bus, for a nod of approval from Matron. 'It's for something bad,' I repeated, in the forlorn hope that Chris would contradict me. 'I know by your voice.'

'This BOY,' Matron said, waving a bundle of letters in front of my startled eyes. 'This BOY. Who is he?'

At least, I thought, recognising them, and recollecting their contents swiftly, at least there's not one 'dirty thing' in them.

'A boy at the Band of Hope, Matron.'

'So that,' Matron had realised, 'is why you're always so keen on the Band of Hope!'

'You'd like him, Matron,' I had assured her. 'He lives

with his Grandfather. He's got blue stockings with yellow tops. He can run like anything. I know you'd like him, if you only knew him!'

Matron, evincing no sign of a passion shared, had locked the letters away in her desk again. 'You can have them, she promised, 'on the day you leave the Orphanage.' But I never got back to the Band of Hope.

'You're getting too old for it now,' Matron had decided. 'It's for children, really. I'd be better teaching you how to use the new Sewing Machine on Friday nights'.

'What punishment?' The others, avid for my destruction, had crowded round me the moment I got back into the scullery. 'What punishment did she say?'

'No punishment,' I assured them casually, rolling up my sleeves to attack the dishes in the sink.

'No punishment!' Their voices rose up in dismay around me.

'No punishment,' I confirmed, skimming enough lather off the water to blow up into fine coloured bubbles. 'But I just can't be bothered going back to the Band of Hope again,' I informed them, keeping an eye on the bubbles that rose to the roof. 'That's just for children. Matron's going to teach me how to use her new Sewing Machine on Friday nights.'

'Her new Sewing Machine?' Surprise mingled with disappointment in their voices.

'Her new Sewing Machine,' I emphasised. Thus was the armour formed.

'You was just never cut out for Service,' my Mistress tried to console me, when I packed my tin trunk again, after six months working on the farm, 'Just never cut out for it.' I silently agreed with her. My first and earliest ambition was to be a Tinker. Maybe I should have stuck to it, for outdoors had always had such a powerful pull on me.

It had taken so little to entice me away from scrubbing the kitchen floor, or doing the weekly wash. A stray dog barking at the back of the house. The whiff of burning gorse, and the men laying it to waste on the slopes of the brae. A hen, slinking past the back door with the proud but furtive look of having returned safely from laying away. And I would be up and off, on a voyage of discovery.

Bent over the ironing board on lamp-lit nights, lost in the book of poetry the dominie had given me. Oblivious to the smell of scorching . . .

Quand tous renait à l'espérance
Et que l'hiver fuit longue de nous
Sous le beau ciel de notre France
Quand l'hirondelle . . .

My Mistress, justifiably enraged, had pointed out that she paid me twenty-six pounds a year to do the housework, not to improve my French. And singe the best tablecloths! There had been no ill-feeling at parting. But the more my Mistress tried to console me, the more a sense of failure assailed me.

'They'll sort something more suitable for you at the Orphanage,' my Mistress tried to assure me. 'I had a word with the Matron. We thought you might do well in one of the big Stores in the Town. You've got a good head on you. Always good at finding and counting the eggs.'

I was not reassured. 'One thing, Matron. I could always count and find the eggs!' Knowing Matron, I knew she would not be impressed by such a brief testimonial.

But at last! At last, though, I had found for myself the Ultimate consolation! I was not going back Pregnant! Even though I had found nobody to be Pregnant with. Except the ploughman on the farm, who sprayed his porridge all over his moustache, because his front teeth were missing. Sex, although its urgings whiles assailed my body, had always to start in my head. It had never even got off to a start, there, with the ploughman.

'Not ME! I'm NOT!' I had hissed, in response to the speculation glimmering in the other girls' eyes. 'I could have been!' I assured them, aware that Virtue unassailed was no Virtue at all. 'I could easily have been. I got plenty of Chances!'

'We have managed to find you another job,' Matron informed me. 'In one of the Town's most exclusive Stores. You'll stay in the Hostel. You should,' she added, appraising me from top to bottom, 'be able to hold on to it. You've got a good memory. And you're quick on your feet. You'll start there as a Messenger!'

. . . Mercury! So essential to the gods. With wings instead of ears. And wings instead of feet . . .

'Your mail, Miss Soutar,' I announced, in my most respectful voice. Delivering my first message to the Buyer in Gardening Implements, down in the basement.

'Call me Madam!' she snarled, grabbing the mail. Without setting eyes on me. As if it was just one of the Garden Gnomes, clustered round her feet, that had handed over her mail.

The idea was ridiculous. But all my life I have suffered from sudden attacks of ridiculous ideas. The Garden Gnomes. And 'Madam'. And the situations and relationships which might occur between them down in the vast secrecy of the basement intrigued me, and kept my mind off my work for the rest of the day. Silken-clad First Sales swooped down on me, like shining black crows. Thrusting back wrongly delivered mail in a silence that shouted their contempt for my inadequacy as a Messenger! Still. Maybe even Mercury had been allowed a mistake or two, before he got acquainted with all the different gods. And I did get Promotion.

Lift Girl. Garbed out in a saxe blue flared frock. With jaunty forage-cap to match. From Household Goods and Haberdashery. To Perfumery and Jewellery. Past Gowns and Mantles. Through the Linen Department. And on up to Carpets and Furniture. I swept my Customers Up. And I swept them Down again. I had such enthusiasm for my Lift that, when I had no Customers at all, I swept myself Up and Down for the sheer exhilaration of it.

Better still, the lone journeys on the Lift gave me time to fantasise a little. The Winter Sales would be coming along. Bringing Matron and the Orphanage girls to buy their new coats at Bargain Prices. Less the discount always allowed for the Orphanage. 'Which floor, Madam?' I would inquire of Matron, as if she was just a Customer I had never set eyes on in my life. As for Chris! Years of a dormitory shared would dissolve in the brief, impersonal look I would cast over Chris! More. When I had delivered them to Gowns and Mantles, I would simply saunter through the department, examining a dress here, adjusting a coat there, to show them I knew What was What. And to impress upon them all my perfect ease in such luxurious surroundings.

It never happened, of course. Or if it did, they must have taken one of the other Lifts. But once imagined, it was just as good as if it had happened.

Like all the other Lift Girls, I looked forward to my next Promotion as Junior Sales. Most of them kept their fingers crossed for Perfumery, Jewellery, Mantles. I kept mine crossed for Window Dressing. Who knew Who might chance along and join the crowd that always clustered round the windows when a transformation was taking place before their very eyes! 'It's just the nude wax models that draws them,' one of the Lift Girls pointed out. 'The Dirty-Minded Things!'

But I felt I could out-match any nude wax model, in a brightly coloured smock, and wide black skirt . . . 'You've got a sure eye for Colour and Contrast,' the Window Display Manager would congratulate me. Admiring from within what all the world was admiring from without . . .

All of us kept our fingers crossed against Promotion to the China Saloon. Despite the fact that it was the most prestigious department in the Store. World-known for its high quality, and high exports. Ruled over by a Madam who was a Martinet and a Perfectionist. Always begowned in deep purple velvet, with hair, high-swept, to match the colour of her gown. The very sight of her approaching was enough to wipe the grins off the girls' faces, and send them scurrying to stand to attention by their Lifts, while Boadicea strode forward into life, towards them.

'Madam in China always gets the first choice of Junior,'

the other girls, hell bent for Perfumery, Jewellery and Mantles, tried to cheer me. 'And she's very choosy. She must have seen something in you,' they added, as if not for the life of them could they see anything!

'Only Horror. And Apprehension,' I thought. And remembered those were things that nobody could see.

I was never promoted beyond Goldfish Bowls. To be written on my heart, like Calais on the heart of Mary Tudor.

From my humble Goldfish Corner, I needed only to cast an appreciative eye in the direction of the display of exquisite figurines. When Madam, tall as she was, would increase in height, stand stock still. And, without uttering one word, would defy me to step within a hundred yards of them.

Even on Saturdays. Busiest of all days, when Madam, with one crack of her fingers, would pulverise all the other Assistants into service, in strict accordance with their seniority.

'Forward, Miss McCabe!'

'Forward, Miss Ellis!'

'Forward, Miss Bain!'

I was never so commanded. And thus 'Miss MacDonald' stood anonymous, and unannounced, in her Goldfish Corner. Glad, indeed, of my anonymity. Grateful that few of the Customers seemed to have much affection for Goldfish. For nothing in the world seemed so awkward to wrap as a Goldfish Bowl. And Perfect Wrapping was high on the list of Madam's definition of a Good China Assistant.

Watching, from a regal distance, my harassed efforts to

wrap, Madam would advance, whip the tattered attempt out of my hands, wrap it perfectly in ten seconds flat, and hand over to the Customer with a smile and a shrug that confided to the Customer, 'You can see what a Fool I've been landed with!'

My Commission—a halfpenny in the pound—must have been the lowest in the Store. I sold few Goldfish Bowls, and, in a desperate attempt to wrap both quickly and perfectly, cracked more than I sold. To add to my troubles, my insteps had fallen. Used to the soft, country roads, the granite pavements had now taken their revenge. I stood in agony. Static in Goldfish Corner. Welling up with self-pity. My feet and legs were my one real vanity. I began to see myself walking flat-footed through the world, for the rest of my days.

My fantasies became fewer. Fading into grim realities . . . Dear God. Keep the Orphanage girls from smashing the dishes. And don't let Matron come within a hundred miles of the China Saloon. Not even when there's a Sale of Seconds . . .

It was only natural for Madam to serve me a week's notice. I was 'a financial loss' to the department. 'Lucky,' one of the girls assured me, to 'get a week's notice'. It was rumoured that Madam had given an Assistant, less fortunate, 'Instant notice', for nothing more than cutting through Wrapping String, instead of unknotting it.

'Is that the best dress you possess?' Madam loomed alarmingly towards me, in the dying hours of my last Saturday in the Store. It was, I admitted, puzzled by her interest in my appearance, when it no longer really mattered. 'We'll have to do something about that, then,' she decided, piloting me towards the Lift of happy memory. 'We can't,' she explained, as we entered the Lift, 'Go to see the Royal Family without a new Dress'.

The blank expression that crossed the Lift Girl's face convinced me that Lifts did have some peculiar influence on those who entered them. I wasn't the only one who fantasised, then? But not. Never in my deepest fantasy had I imagined Myself and Madam on visiting terms with the Royal Family.

'They've arrived at Balmoral for the Summer,' Madam in China confided to Madam in Gowns. Ladies both. On easy, intimate terms with the Royal Family. Familiar with their comings and goings. 'They're later, this year,' Madam in Gowns reflected, 'Owing no doubt to the Regatta. Still,' she added, 'we should get a close look, when they pass by to Crathie Kirk.'

Nobody wanted a Goldfish Bowl in my last hour in the Store. A benison that gave me time to ponder the enigma that was Madam. Aloof once more. She had never spoken more than twenty words to me. Yet she had just let me choose, and herself paid for, a new dress. And she was taking me, tomorrow, Sunday, to see the Royal Family pass by.

'I don't know what she can do now,' I had heard Madam whisper to Madam in Gowns, as they had searched their way along the dress rails. I didn't know myself. There must be something I could do.

'Live, Madam,' I thought, aware for the first time that Madam was quite old! 'Live, dear Madam, till I find that something.'

PART IX

LATER POEMS

ELEGY

I did not know that you were dead:
A granite tomb-stone told me so,
Verified that Evelyn Mary
Died long years ago.
Too young for wine, for broken bread,
Barred from Communion with the Host,
We were released, set free to go
When voices rose to paraphrase
. . . ‘ ’Twas on that night when doomed to know.’
We didn’t then
Yet. We were familiar with the dead.
We knew each name carved out in stone.
Played hide and seek among their tombs
While others mourned to atone.
I’ve chanced upon your ‘Hidie’ Place
But cannot find you.

UNTITLED

Not always does time cancel beauty,
Nor wars and sorrows rob it of its flowers.
My mother has not an accent,
A look, a smile, an act,
That does not sharply touch my heart.
Ah! if I were a painter,
I would not ask of Raphael his divine brush.
I should like to exchange life for Life,
To give her all the vigour of my years.

SPELL BINDERS

I miss the ancient mariners,
the tellers of tall tales
who clustered round the Close Mouth
of my childhood,
clutching at me,
unwilling to set but one believer free.
I miss their sounds of Verily,
the vows that proved it so
        —As sure as Death—
        —As God's my Judge—
        —May I drop Dead—
the ebb and flow
and tides of talk receding in a sigh
        —But you're owre young tae ken
        the way it was
        the things that happened
        then—
Yet
Youth was no impediment,
'twas then I knew
a tale is still a tale
be it false or true.

SOMEBODY

Ye can tell when somebody is Somebody
or thinks they are.
Ye can tell
the sett o' the heid held heich
an flung well back.
This is the chield wha taks the opposition stance,
aye mair nor ready tae heist it on tae you,
should you by dire mischance
hover in view.
Bit I kent a chield wi' sense o' purpose
in his fit,
planked firmly doon atop the bar's brass rail
like he was moulded on t'ilt
up tae his elbow.
'Nip ana Hauf' was aye his shout
on Dole Day.
Faith! He was Somebody then,
a chield ye'd hardly notice ither days,
cut doon tae pint-size,
checkin' his change.

PART X

REUNION

REUNION

(Seated at table, she is signing copies of her books. Rattle at letterbox. She rises and collects delivery of large envelope. Returns to table. Opens envelope. A photograph of recent school Reunion of primary class circa 1926. She studies it)

(As to self) Sixty years on. We've worn weel.

(She rises. Crosses to bureau. Searches. Takes primary school photograph from bureau. As she straightens up, she catches glimpse of herself in ornamental mirror above bureau. She studies her reflection, feeling and touching contours of her face)

(To reflection) Auld face. Poor auld face. Maskin' that young lass that still lives somewhere inside you. That's the worst thing about growing auld, your body ages lang before your spirit fades. I never see the young lasses racin' laughin' past me but I feel like protestin', shoutin' to them: I could run as fast as you, once upon a time.

(Peers closer at her image in the mirror. Touches her facial contours again)

(As to self) Good God! So much for moisturising cream! It did nothing for You!

(She returns to table. Dials telephone)

Isa! Thanks. I've got the Reunion photo. It arrived when I was signing the books I promised the class as a thank you for their bonnie gesture.

(She listens)

The pleasure was mine. Isa, to tell ye the truth, I didna ken what was the greatest honour, the Doctorate or the Reunion Lunch the class gave me for the Doctorate.

(She listens)

The thing that touched me maist. When you rose and gave the toast, 'To Doctor Kesson,' you said. Fan the class stood up, they were as uncomfortable wi' ma new title as I was masel! 'To Jessie,' they said. I loved them for that. Dear and homely and sweet. As if I was ane o' their ain—at last.

(Puts phone down quietly. Sits, thinks for brief space. Lifts Reunion photo. Addresses it, intimately)

No. You werena ane o' their ain. You could never be that. Sair as you would like to be. And sair as you aye wanted to be. You used the auldest trick in the world to mak sure you werena left oot, at the school. You became the court jester o' the class.

(Grins. As she looks across at Doctorate photo and addresses it)

Better folk than you have done that! Will Somers, Henry Eighth's fool, did the same thing! That's why he keepit his heid on his shoulders. He could aye mak the King laugh.

(Subdued. Reflective)

You'd forgotten a' aboot that till the day o' the Reunion. You hoped that the class had forgotten. For you didna feel proud o' yersel when ye mindit on't.

'I envy you,' Chrissie Lamont said to you. 'You've done

so much,' she said. 'You've seen so much. And I've done nothing very much with my life, never really been awa fae the district in my life.'

(She picks up Reunion photograph, studies it. Addresses it)

Ah, Chrissie lass, I envied you. I envied you a' on the day o' the Reunion, still close thegither. Nae far awa'. Or still on the farms your great-grandfathers had worked. And your grandchildren would work on. You kent who you were. And where you were. And that's a fine thing to ken. And I havena seen that much o' the world, Chrissie, the odd coach tour, and it's nae up to much. Slippin' off your sheen to rest your feet—and hell and a' tae get them on again. Because your feet have swollen up. And the courier harryin' ye here and there before you've got time to hae a right look at onything! Ah, Chrissie, what you did see o' the world was seen in comfort and in style, I'm sure o' that! You dinna need to envy me. I've had no continuing city, as the Bible says. Still . . .

(Brief, silent reflection)

I wadna have had it otherwise. I've never gone under a new roof yet without wondering if I'd like to die under that roof. And aye the answer is NO! There you are, you see; it gives me a kind o' feeling of immortality. An illusion, it's true, but a fine thing to hae. The poet said it a' for me:

For good undone
For gifts mis-spent
For resolutions vain
It's rather late to think of this
I know.

But I'd live the same life over
If I had to live again
And the chances are I'll go
Where most men go.

(Looks again at photograph. Reflects)

Aye, Chrissie. You had other things I'd hae likit. Beauty. You was the flower o' the flock at the school. And still bonnie in your auld age.

(Lays down photograph. Searches table for school photograph of class, taken sixty years ago. Remembers it's on top of the bureau. Rises, goes to bureau to retrieve it. Looks at mirror. Addresses it)

Attractive! Folk have said I'm attractive. A second-rate word. A poor substitute for beauty.

(She fingers and examines her hair. Reflects)

Maybe I overdid it wi' that new brand o' hair colouring. 'Medium Ash Brown' the bottle said. It turned out carroty red on me! Maggie Firth was the only one to comment on that at the Reunion. She was aye observant, was Maggie. 'You used to be Moosie Broon when you was at the school,' she reminded me—as if I needed remindin'.

(She runs fingers through her hair again. Reflects)

Carroty red! What was it the dominie used to say? 'Stick to the old if it is good. Try the new. It may be better,' The kind o' advice that leaves ye wi' a dilemma! You should have stuck to Medium Ash Brown.

(She picks primary class photograph off bureau and returns to sit at table. She studies photograph. Reflects)

I recognise you a'. I can put a name to every face. Strange that: at the Reunion last week it took us a while to recognise each ither again. Nae wonder. Sixty years is a lang time. I can even mind the clothes you wore. And their colours.

(Looks closely at photograph. Reflects)

You've got on your Mackenzie Tartan kilt, Liz Gartly. I aye wanted a kilt. Feelin' entitled to it. Bein' the only one in the class wi' a Hieland name! I prayed for a kilt. The wrong thing to pray for, the Matron said. Grace. Mercy. And Truth, she said, were the right things to pray for. I never bothered. Grace, Mercy and Truth were things you couldna see. Even if you prayed for them, you wadna ken if you'd got them or no. That's the kind o' prayer that gives God a loophole. I got my kilt, though. It was the first thing I bought out o' my first month's wages at the farm. I seldom wore it, though. By the time I got it, I felt too auld to wear it. It gave me pleasure for all that. I liked to spread it across my bed and look at its colours.

(Studies photograph. Reflects)

You're gone noo; the war took you. And you. It decorated you though. Sergeant William Blane DFM. I read it years ago in the paper. Unchancy things, honours. I thought to masel' at the time, the pilot in your bomber would have gotten the DFC. And the level o' your mutual bravery would have been the same. The only difference, ane got a medal, the other a cross. The country postie that works hard and weel at his job for thirty years could end up with the BEM. If the chield that produces this programme sticks it oot for thirty years, he could end up wi' the OBE. I canna understand it. Still . . .

(Looks closely at photograph)

Still, Sergeant William Blane, DFM (Posthumous): you

didna live to ken o' your honour. But we kent. And were proud o' and proud for you.

(Looks across at Doctorate photograph. Addresses it)

You canna grumble! You got an honour yersel'. Even Virginia Woolf, who refused all University Honours, admitted that if she did accept an honour, it would be a University one. Nae a Queen's ane.

(She returns to study of school photograph. Reflects)

Maud Sherrif—she wasna at the Reunion. Dead? They would have mentioned it.

(Dials telephone)

Isa! Is Maud Sherrif dead?

(Listens)

No! She wasna at the Reunion. Did ye invite her?

(Listens)

Ye did! She didna want to come!

(Listens)

Because she didna like me!

(Listens)

She couldna stand me! I never kent that! I never did onything tae her.

(Listens)

(Vehemently) I'm nae carin', of coorse, I'm nae carin'. I couldna care less whether Maud Sherrif likes me or no. It's just—

(Puts hand over telephone mouthpiece)

(As to self) It's just everybody likes to be likit.

(On telephone) Could I call you back, Isa. There's somebody at the door.

(Puts down receiver. Leans back in chair. Reflects, nonplussed)

It's a strange thing. I've aye had a kind o' respect for the folk that dinna like me. I aye feel they can see through me, warts an' a'.

(Picks up school photograph again, studies it. Reflects)

Miss Inch. There you are. I'd a letter a year or two back fae my best frien' at school. 'Miss Inch had her favourites,' she wrote. 'After all, we couldna all be farmers' or ministers' daughters.' The quine was right! We couldna! I wasna ane o' Miss Inch's favourites. Or thocht I wasna. Though, come to think o't, she couldna have held my father's status against me. For she didna ken wha he was. Or what he was. Nae mair than I kent masel'! Mind you!

(Pauses; grins)

Lots o' folk are concerned aboot that, though it never bothers me. I was up in my hame town nae lang ago. Twa o' my auldest frien's had 'discovered' a father for me. The problem was, they'd each discovered a different father, wi' one thing in common. Baith assured me that he had once been a Very Prominent Man in the Town. Who was I tae quibble or tak offence? It's nae a'body, legal or otherwise, that has the choice o' twa Prominent Men for a father. Miss Inch would have been impressed.

(Studies photograph)

Aye, Miss Inch, you had often a sharp edge to your tongue. BUT she was a grand teacher. I had great respect for her as a teacher. I was eight when I cam tae that school, and tae her class. I had a letter wi' a' my particulars to be given to her. For days after I cam tae her class, she never called me by my name. Just aye 'Girl MacDonald'. I thocht she'd lost my name. Or had forgotten it.

(Studies photograph. Reflects)

AND, Missy Inch, you'd gotten a sarcastic edge to your tongue whiles. We were eight years auld when you started us off sewin', beginning wi' a lap bag to haud our sewin'. My lap bag never held mine. It took me seven years to finish it. Week after week, I'd tae unpick a' the cross stitches I'd sewn the week afore. I just dreaded when you handed our sewin' out. Haudin' my lap bag up for the inspection o' the class. Who is the owner of this disgusting object? you'd ask, kennin' fine it was me. True enough, it did look like a dirty dish cloot. It couldnae look onything else. It was sair mishandled wi' a' the years o' unpickin'. Still . . .

(Pause to reflect)

I mind one year at the Village Flower Show, I was wanderin' roon the marquee lookin' at a' the exhibits. I couldna believe ma een when I got to the School section. There was a First Prize Red Card on one o' my school essays. And a First Prize Red Card on an envelope I'd addressed in a lesson at the school. I couldna believe it. For I'd never entered onything. Each entry cost sixpence. And I hadna got sixpence.

(Looks at photograph)

I realised that you must have entered them for me. And peyed the entry fees yersel'. I was five shillings rich that day. So, Missy Inch, there was anither side to ye, but I didna discover it till the day o' the Flower Show.

(She lifts up photograph of Reunion, compares it to photo of class of 1926)

(As to self) Then and now. The hairdresser got a bit o' trade on the day o' the Reunion.

(Reflects)

I havena been inside a hairdresser's half a dizzen times in my life. I aye cam oot a' curls and frizz. Of course it didna suit me! My face is too strong for curls. I just went over the top a'thegither! Slappin' on moisturising cream and goin' on a diet a fortnight afore the Reunion. Flab aye goes to my midriff. That was my biggest problem. I couldna mak up my mind what to wear. It bein' such a special occasion.

I discovered a strange thing, Isa. Aboot masel', I mean. For years, when I was young, when claes are important to ye, I'd nae decisions to mak. Haein' nae wardrobe to speak o'. Ye ken what I mean. One thing on, and the other in the wash. Noo I've gotten mair claes than I'll live tae wear oot, but nae the same pleasure in wearin' them as I wad have had, when I was young. Same thing wi' money. I used tae worry because I hadna enough. Noo that I've got mair then enough, my worry is how to haud on to it. There's a lesson there somewhere, but I dinna ken what it is.

ONYWEY, in the end, I decided to wear my purple suit—the 'season's colour', supposed to be. But, wi' me bein' on the diet, the skirt was hingin' on me. I just didna look my best.

Aye! You and me aye argued about that, Isa. Brains or beauty. I'd aye raither have been beautiful. Just think o't, Isa, real beauties. Model quines and chorus girls married into the aristocracy. Some o' them just becam mistresses?

(Laughs)

I canna help laughin', Isa. I was richt confused aboot mistresses at the school. Romantic aboot them. We were on Shakespeare at the time, sonnets and things—'Mistress mine, where are you roving?'—'Lines to his Mistress's Eyebrows'. Till ae day, a Sunday it was, the matron and the servant were speaking aboot a scandal they'd read in the Sunday paper, a divorce. My lugs, aye finely attuned to grown-ups' conversations, heard the matron sayin', 'He'll never marry her! A man never marries his mistress'. I just couldna believe that mistresses were scandalous. But then, I was a Romantic, then.

(Picks up Reunion photograph. Looks silently at it. Reflects, addressing it)

My 'lad', Alick. It wasna surprisin' that, at fifteen, I set my heirt on you. The wonder was that you set your heirt on me. For you was wondrous bonnie. You could have had your pick o' the lassies at the school. *(As to self)*

> But our love was stronger far than the love
> Of many far older than we
> Many far wiser than we
> And neither the angels in
> Heaven above
> Nor the demons down under the sea
> Could ever dismember my soul
> from the soul . . .

That's how it was for me, Alick. In my last year at the school. It was as if I'd burst into blossom. The one time I felt as beautiful as I aye wanted to be. I excelled at my lessons. Because you was there to see. I wad run like a hare if you was watchin'. To show you how fleet I was on my feet.

And you, Alick? I think it was the same for you. You could aye score a goal when I was watchin'. And speed doon Barclay's Brae on your bike wi' nae hands on the handle-bars, if I was lookin'. We were like birds. Goin' through their matin' rituals in the Spring. We never got further than the rituals. And I was grateful for that when I met you and your wife at the Reunion. I could look you baith in the face. There nivir had been ony houghmagandie behind the school bike shed.

'Pleased to meet you,' your wife said. 'Alick's often spoken about you.' There was things you couldna have spoken aboot, Alick. Because you didna ken.

You'll mind, of coorse, about Temperance. The Band of Hope in the Kirk Hall on Friday nights. The walk to the Hall was oor trystin' place. Oor trystin' time. But you never kent the struggle I had tae keep that tryst. And it wasnae a struggle against 'the angels in Heaven above' NOR 'the demons down under the sea'. But just against the Matron. She wasna keen on lettin' me to the Band of Hope. I could understand that. She kent there was little chance o' me drinkin' masel tae death while under her care. But a fifteen-year-auld quine on an unchaperoned twa mile walk on a country road on a Friday nicht set her imagination workin' against my love-stricken sel'. She could hardly refuse the Minister's request that I 'join the Band of Hope'. But she did a' she could to limit my attendance.

'The Band of Hope only when it doesn't rain.'

It never rained so much on Friday nichts as it did in my last year at the school. I'd get oot o' my bed on Friday mornin's as sune as dawn was comin' in. Stan'in' at the window in my bare feet on the cauld linoleum. Searchin' the sky. Interpretin' the weather. I kent the contours o' clouds. Their darkness. Their density. I could sniff oot rain on the wind on the road to the school. I evoked the elements themselves wi' chants o' childhood memory.

Rainie rainie rattlestanes
Dinna rain on me
Rain on Johnnie Groat's hoose
Far across the sea.

I tried to get roon God Himsel'.

Dear God, ye can let it rain every nicht except Friday nicht. If it be Thy will . . .

You didna ken that, Alick.

Sixty years on, fan we met again at the Reunion, I looked at you. And you looked at me. I'm sure we both saw the same thing. The flooers o' the forest werena deid. They were faded, nae langer in bonnie bloom.

(She rises. Gathers photographs together, places them inside bureau. Stands silent for a few seconds)

(As to self) The poet has a word for it all . . .

A lass cam' sabbin'
 Tae my brink
Tae dip her hand
 An' wishin', drink.
'Oh water, water,
 Gi'e tae me
This wish I wish,
 Or else I dee!'

REUNION

Back cam' the lass
 Years efter-hand,
An peered again
 At my dancin' sand.
'I mind,' she said,
 'O' drinkin' here,
But—Losh keep me,
 What did I speir?'

PART XI

COLD IN COVENTRY

COLD IN COVENTRY

EMMA knew the Admittance Room well. Years of polishing its every nook and cranny had forged an intimacy between herself and the Room.

Fourteen now, she had been eight when Madam Superintendent of the Training Institution for Destitute Girls had put her under the charge of an older girl who had 'instructed' her in what was to become her specific weekly task, the 'thoroughing out' of the Admittance Room. Once a week, for seven years, she had 'turned out' this room. She found herself counting the times. Fifty-two weeks in a year. Seven times fifty-two, three hundred and sixty-four times . . .

The room hadn't changed, she thought, gazing round it. But then it didn't have long enough to change. She had been away from it for only three months in her 'first situation'.

Days though, rising up in her memory of those seven years, when the Room took on a more ominous title and became the Re-Admission Room. She had never known it—until now—in *that* guise, but had shared with fifty other girls in the Institution avid speculation on what happened to a girl returned In Disgrace to a Room which could so swiftly change its name and its purpose.

The Summonsing Bell for Morning Prayers clanged through her thoughts. It would be followed by girls rushing past her door and along the corridor to Chapel. If she was blind, if she had to stay forever in this room she would never be lonely. Not as long as hearing lasted and she could hear the Summonsing Bells ring out the divisions of each day's duties.

Listening to the sounds of the girls' approaching footsteps she knew that they wouldn't open the door of the Room. They would halt outside it. She knew that too. To savour for a brief moment the relief of being on the *right* side of safety.

Pray for Peter
Pray for Paul.

She mocked after their disappearing backs.

Never pray for ME at all!!!

The small gesture of defiance smiled her. Closing the door quietly the sound of the singing Morning Prayers rose faintly from the distance. She had no need to hear its *words.* She knew them. Taking up the Prayer itself, she sang it as if she was still amongst them in the Chapel . . .

Father of all we bow to Thee
Who dwellest in Heaven adored

Forever hallowed be Thy Name
By all beneath the skies
From day to day we humbly own
The hand that feeds us still
Our sins before Thee we confess
O may they be forgiven . . .

Emma's sins would not be forgiven. At least not by Madam. The reason for her dismissal from her job had arrived before herself. To be read out by Madam . . .

Kingston Manor
Wivesfield
Sussex

10 April 1895

My cook informs me that Emma Gartly was a pleasant girl to have in the kitchen, but her mind was seldom on her duties. As she is the SECOND girl I have employed from your institution whose work has now proved unsatisfactory, I have no option but to withdraw my Patronage.

The loss of a Patron . . . *That* Emma knew would be unforgivable.

'Do you *agree* with the *Reason* for your dismissal?'

'Yes Madam.'

'Have you anything else to say for yourself?'

'No Madam.'

Plenty to say. But there were no words that would justify her failure to Madam. Maybe, she thought, trying to clarify it in her own mind . . . Maybe if she had been a tablemaid . . . She had fancied being a tablemaid after seeing the pictures of the former girls in their uniforms. Smart, tablemaids had looked. White streamers hanging down from the crowns of their caps to their shoulders. Or even an Under Housemaid. Clean in their white all-embracing aprons. But—scullery-maid—Emma had felt so dirty all the time—A dirty, greasy girl. Bent always over a wooden sink. Half hidden inside a big oilskin apron. Or down on her knees in a bag apron scrubbing the stone flags of the Kitchen floor. Everybody rushing past her as if they hadn't seen her. As if she didn't exist. Flinging everything that was dirty into a sink that seldom seemed to be empty. In the three months in her Situation she had felt caught up in a whir of Apology . . . Bent under a perpetual vow of Atonement.

Sorry, Cook. I didn't know you wanted ME to *chop* the Parsley.

I'll do it straight away.

I thought I *had* taken *all* the eyes out of the potatoes. I'll go over them again. Won't take me a minute.

The Cod's Heads. I gave them to the Cat. I didn't *know* you wanted them for the staff's fish soup.

No Cook. I wouldn't want THAT. I'd never want the Cat to choke on the Cod's heads. I like the Cat. I'll remember next time.

Cook was right in her warnings. 'You better had remember my Girl!' Right too in her forecast that Emma 'Hadn't the makings of a scullery-maid'. No wonder Cook 'didn't know what was to become of her'. Emma didn't know herself.

She had been shying away from speculation on Madam's ultimate decision on her fate. Warily touching the alternatives rising to the surface of her mind.

It wouldn't be the Workhouse. You had to be Pregnant to be sent to the Workhouse. The Reformatory? She hadn't been Bad enough for the Reformatory. If she had been a Boy from the Boys' Division, it could have been a Training Ship. Or away on some other ship to work on a farm in Canada. Options for the Boys in Disgrace opened wide horizons in her mind. Sea and space. Time to recover yourself on a long voyage to Destination and Doom. Maybe, maybe they wouldn't bother taking you back In Disgrace all the way from Canada. A further Period of Training? Madam might decide on *that.* Not *here* though. You'd been Out In The World, as Madam described it. She didn't want the other girls to be 'influenced' by what you'd discovered Out In The World.

As in other critical moments in her short life Emma began to manipulate time. Caught up in a warp of her making. Clutching briefly at remembered safety. Just three short months ago she was—safe—in this Room. Cleaning it out. In a day that was ordinary. The Room itself hadn't changed. The huge Tract on the wall above the marble mantel. Signed by St Paul, it still exhorted all who set eyes on it. 'Little Children Love Ye One Another'. It was the change in *her* circumstances that altered her attitude towards it. St Paul had got it wrong. Had come to the wrong address. The girls had never 'loved' one another. Self-preservation had prevented it. *Madam's* approval was

ALL. They would have shot their grandmothers if such a dastardly deed would have won them Madam's Approval.

The Breakfast Bell ringing out brought speculation to an end. Prepared this time for the rush of girls pausing and passing the door of the Room, Emma was ready to pounce. To deprive them of smugness. Flinging open the door to confront them:

'Look at me. Take a *good* look. I haven't turned into a monster.'

Taken by surprise they scattered. Scuttling past the door. 'I'm NOT,' she called after them, 'I'm Not Pregnant You Lousy LOT.'

Still, she had to admit to herself when the brief period of derring do had faded, she herself had acted exactly the same on the day any girl sacked from her job returned In Disgrace. A day that became High Lit. Lifting them all up out of the monotonous routine of ordinary days. The girl's failure making the others feel 'The Good Ones'. A rare feeling. One to be savoured. Closing ranks. Making excuses to run round to the laundry past the window of the Room to get a quick peek at the girl inside it. Feeling she must have changed. Must carry the imprint of failure on her face.

Times though, times slipping into mind when Emma had been in high favour with the other girls. At night—that safest time—in their small, black iron beds, the 'covering' defences of the day cast off, set aside with their Combinations and Liberty Bodices.

'Tell us a story, Emma.'

Their pleas rising up in her mind.

'A poem Emma. A poem from the book.'

The sources of her stories still stood intact in the large, mahogany bookcase. Fingering through them . . .

> Jessica's First Prayer. Christy's Old Organ. Eric.
> Little By Little. Saturday's Child.

All stories which implied that it was better to die young and Saved, than to grow old and become a Sinner, which Madam sometimes seemed to think they had signs of becoming.

'A sad poem, Emma. "The Orphan Boy"! I'll let *You* dry next time we're on Washing Up if you say "The Orphan Boy".'

Strange, Emma thought, putting *Poems of Victorian Childhood* back in its place in the bookcase. Its shiny leather cover still slippery to her touch. Strange, the girls seldom wept for themselves. But often shed tears for a boy in a book.

They *couldn't* have forgotten. They could *never* have forgotten *that* . . .

They *had* forgotten. Emma recognised that the moment Agnes Bradley opened the door of the Room. Facing each other in a second's silence that spanned a decade of shared childhood with no acknowledgement of former allegiance. That hurt. It hurt more than *Madam* could. And Madam *knew* it. A girl was officially appointed on a Day like this, as her Go Between.

'INVENTORY.' Agnes set the Form down on the table. 'Madam has checked your trunk.' In her official role Agnes's voice had taken on the sound of Madam. 'One morning cap missing. One apron beyond reasonable repair.' It was only when Agnes reached the door that she sounded like Agnes. Known of old.

'*You'll* have some *explaining* to do. It had better be good.'

Missing cap. Torn apron. Wear and Tear? Not a good enough reason. Emma hadn't been long enough away from the Institution to claim for Wear and Tear. The truth? Emma grappled for words that could contain the truth.

It was the Boot Boy, Madam. Always on the look-out for me in his shed behind the Kitchen Garden, when I'd run out for more parsley and spring onions and things. He grabbed me from behind one day. Pinched my cap and wouldn't give it back unless I gave him a kiss.

The very thought of Madam's reaction to a kiss, and a Boy—Boot or otherwise, flung truth straight out of the windows in Emma's mind. Though truth it was. There had been no relationship on *Emma's* part with the Boot Boy. *Cook* would never have stood for *that*. She didn't like the Boot Boy. 'Another of her Ladyship's Charitables,' she said of him. 'From that Barnardo's.' Cook couldn't forgive him for not wiping his boots properly on the scraper at the back door . . . 'dragging all the Dirt into my Kitchen,' she complained.

Once, Emma remembered, having herself discovered something about the deficiency of the boot scraper. Only once had she had a sudden impulse to speak up in defence of the Boot Boy.

It's his boots, Cook. Like my boots. Too big for the scraper. They don't take a right grip. They just slide along it.

Emma had not yet been exhorted to Beware of Pity.

Nor had she lived long enough yet to think that the *real* danger lay in NOT having pity. So. Mindful of Cook's feeling towards the Boot Boy, as sole Counsel for the Defence Emma had kept silent about the scraper.

'My cap got lost in the laundry, Madam,' she would say to Madam. 'Things were always getting lost or torn there.' The lie would be more acceptable than the truth. No *wonder* Madam often accused them of lying. They *were* liars. Of a kind. They needed something, somebody to boast about. The kind of parents they would like to have had. The homes they would like to have lived in. Emma didn't suppose for a *minute* that the girls believed her claim to having been 'Born in a Big House'. Though it was true as far as it went. She simply omitted to mention that it was the Workhouse. They accepted each others' lies. They had need of them.

O give thanks
O give thanks
O give thanks unto the Lord
For He is gracious and His mercy
Endureth
Endureth forever . . .

The girls' voices sounding up from the Chapel brought breakfast to an end. Bringing to her mind their *own* version—

There is a happy land
Far far away
Where we get bread and marg

Three times a day
Ham and eggs we never see
Nor sugar in our tea
And we are gradually
Fading away . . .

For the first time since she had entered the Room, Emma felt the pain of Outwithness as the girls rushed laughing past the door for recreation in the walled Bleaching Green. Free to themselves to be at one with each other. Full of shared secrecies. Flinging themselves down on their backs. Their long, black-stockinged legs scything the air. Convulsed with laughter as they chorused a song of Protest against the rigidity of their days.

. . . HOLY MOSES
I am dying
Just a word before I go
Put the cat on the table
Put the Poker up its HOL . . . Y MOSES . . .

'Your breakfast,' Agnes announced, clamping down the tray before distancing herself from the table. 'AND Madam will see you in her Office at ten o'clock.'

'I'm not hungry,' Emma slid the tray along the table. 'I don't want Breakfast.'

'*That's* up to YOU.' Agnes shrugged. 'You *know* the Rules. They haven't changed. No dinner till you've eaten your breakfast.'

Mindful of how food was so often on their minds and Madam's puzzled claim that she 'could find no bottom to their hunger', Emma decided that her recently acquired knowledge of food—Out In The World—could not fail to 'rattle' Agnes . . .

'I have NEVER been hungry since I left *here*,' she claimed, with truth on her side.

'Cook gave me plenty of Tastes. She said I needed "Feeding Up". I got left-overs from Upstairs. And seconds when there was any left. AND I *always* got to scrape the Cake Mixture from the bottom of her Baking Bowl!'

'Is THAT,' Agnes asked when she reached the door, 'is THAT why you've got FAT?'

'I'm NOT,' Emma shouted before Agnes could reach the end of the Corridor, 'I'm not Pregnant. I got PLENTY of CHANCES!'

Chances. *That* would slay Agnes. It would kill her. Emma stood relishing her small moment of triumph.

Chances whispered about. Speculated upon. Anticipated for that Out In The World time which beckoned them all. The clothes they'd choose for themselves. Frocks that didn't have to last till that long time when you '*grew* into them'. Dances. Boys. Not Pregnancy itself. Never Pregnancy. You *knew* what would happen if you were Pregnant. But the Preludes to Pregnancy. Ah. *That* was a different thing. Being in love. A state much discussed. Deeply desired. CHANCES!!!

It was on the long walk to Madam's Office, that Emma, walking several paces behind Agnes as her lack of status now required, took an old escape route into the realms of prayer and fantasy.

Dear God make me be Back On A Visit. All Dressed-Up Head Housemaid. With a photo of me in my Uniform to give Madam to hang on the wall. *And* make Agnes Bradley be Back Pregnant.

It was when they came to that sudden halt at the door of Madam's Office with its warning sign Knock Before Entering, that fantasy and prayer fled from Emma's mind and reality took over. A girl In Disgrace *never* came back ON A VISIT.

COMMENTARY

General

Many of Kesson's quotations have proved hard to trace. Unattributed quotations in her work may often be of her own authorship: evidence in various letters and radio scripts indicates she often quietly quoted herself.

One example: a poem quoted in 'Railway Journey', 'The Childhood' and 'Somewhere Beyond', ('I wad hae made a wudden horse /Oot o' ilka aiken tree') bears close resemblance to a poem called 'Aiken Tree' which she published in 'Four Poems' in *The Scots Magazine* in December 1942. This poem appears in this *Companion* three times, in different dramas, and each time the quote is slightly different. This is a characteristic of Kesson's writing.

I
Early Stories

Railway Journey

First published anonymously in two parts in *North-East Review* in October and November 1941. An editorial comment reads: 'This true story of a young girl is a social document of real importance'. Written early in Kesson's cottar career, it is the first surviving account of her fractured childhood, and the pull between her early childhood self in the Elgin slums and countryside and her second self, developed in a more ordered and cleaner, but less loving and intimate, upbringing at the orphanage in Skene, in Aberdeenshire.

Already the author seems acutely aware of the problems of forging a coherent identity out of her past, and she has already seized on the journey between the places as an effective image, as she did later in *The White Bird Passes*.

P3 'beauteous things' from Robert Bridges' poem 'I love all beauteous things'.

P3 'all along a dirtiness . . .' adapted from Kipling's 'The 'Eathen'.

Ferm Deem

First published in *The Scots Magazine*, volume 44, in 1946. Kesson's first job, which she undertook most unwillingly, was as a 'kitchie deem' on a farm near the orphanage at Skene.

She was very unsuccessful, and eventually sent back to the orphanage. There was no ill will, and her mistress tried to console her for her failure. See the final story,

'Cold in Coventry', for the lasting impact this made on her.

In 'Ferm Deem', unusually written in Scots throughout, she used her all-too-real experience of the job—and an imaginary character, the simple-minded, unloved and unlovely Rose—in a plot which underlines the misery of the lives of ill-used kitchie deems of her day, and the direct relationship between the degree of that misery and the personal qualities of the farmers' wives who employed them.

II
Selected Early Poems

A Scarlet Goon

Kesson wrote 'A Scarlet Goon' for the BBC in 1945, her first for-radio writing. It was first published in *The Scots Magazine*, 1946. Kesson bitterly regretted not being given the chance of a university education. The local details here are all about Aberdeen, her local university. She did receive a scarlet gown in the end, awarded an Honorary Doctorate of Letters at Aberdeen in 1987, at the installation of Sir Kenneth Alexander as Chancellor of the University, a quietly triumphant and healing occasion commemorated in 'Reunion'. Sir Kenneth wrote to me in 1996:

'I read *The White Bird Passes* when I was teaching at Aberdeen in the late fifties, and was very impressed by it. I remember Charlie Allan singing the praises of Jessie's work to me some fifteen years later, and on reading more my admiration increased. Jessie had not then been given the recognition she deserved, and I was glad of the opportunity to have the University honour such a fine writer and splendid human being with such strong roots in our part of Scotland.'

Blaeberry Wood

A favourite poem of Kesson's, commemorating an ecstatic experience of nature in her Elgin days. It was first published in *The Scots Magazine*, 1942, and on several other occasions, under different titles.

Fir Wud

Published in *The Scots Magazine* in 1945. Neil Gunn so much admired this poem that he sent the writer a postcard, which she remembered as reading: 'I have just read "Fir Wud" in *Scots Magazine*. A first class poem judged by highest standards. If you would continue to write poetry of that quality you would do more for Scottish literature than by any amount of prose.'

This led to an invitation to visit him, and to his recommending her to inherit his 'Country-Dweller's Year' column in the magazine. She happily complied, with monthly articles by 'Ness Macdonald' (her maiden name) throughout 1946.

To Nan Shepherd

Published in *North-East Review*, 1945. The author was given as 'J.K.'

Dr Nan Shepherd, novelist, poet and academic (1893–1981), met Kesson on a train in 1941, and was instrumental in encouraging her to write. They remained friends until Shepherd's death.

Autumn Dyke

Another ecstatic nature poem, 'Autumn Dyke' was published in *The Scots Magazine*, volume 45, in 1946. It is a poem Kesson often quoted in radio scripts. She used it in 'Apples be Ripe: an Aberdeenshire Autumn', which was directed by Elizabeth Adair, where a slightly different version of the poem introduces the programme (1946). She used it again in 'The Gleaners: an Autumnal Reverie', which was directed by Elizabeth Adair in October 1948, Kesson's poem here rubbing shoulders with Burns, Wordsworth and the Book of Ruth.

III
Early Radio Work

Anybody's Alley: Some Memories of a Scottish Childhood

After a very full year of periodical publishing in 1946, Kesson turned her formidable energies to (better-paid) work for the BBC. She began with short, often autobiographical pieces, such as 'Anybody's Alley'. Described as 'memories of a Scottish childhood', it was first broadcast in the Scottish Home Service on 14 October 1947. Kesson herself was the 'story-teller', and the programme was produced by Elizabeth Adair in Aberdeen.

Adair was Kesson's first producer, and the pair collaborated closely and successfully for some years. Neither a play nor a simple talk, this piece is a re-creation for radio of some of the Lane childhood that would be celebrated in *The White Bird Passes*. Annie Frigg of *The White Bird Passes* here makes her first appearance (as Grigg). Here it is her death that fills the child with fear for her mother's mortality: the alarmingly close-to-home suicide of the other local prostitute Mysie Walsh only happens in the novel. This piece, like many others, shows Kesson's fascination with larger-than-life characters, and with the wild social life of the Lane.

P36 'But she was beautiful. . .' from Shelley's 'The Witch of Atlas'. In *The White Bird Passes*, this quotation is applied to Janie's mother Liza (p119).

The Childhood

See Introduction. This was broadcast in October 1949, produced by Elizabeth Adair in Aberdeen. For clarity, I have called this 'The Childhood (1)'. The second, quite different, play, which I label 'The Childhood (2)', was produced in 1952, and was also extremely popular and repeated many times. In 'The Childhood (1)', Bryden Murdoch played Daniel the man, and Kesson herself was Kate.

P52 'There is not in the wide world' from Thomas Moore's 'The Meeting of the Waters'.

P53 'Kernon's a Jessy'—an unusual hint of self-identification.

P63 'Yet it was not that Nature . . .' from 'The Meeting of the Waters' again.

We Can't Go Back

First broadcast in *Woman's Hour* on 1 January 1957, when

Kesson was Inspector in Charge of the Cowley Recreational Institution in Brixton. The talk was later chosen for a *Woman's Hour* anthology volume. The poem quoted at the end is Violet Jacob's 'The Howe o' the Mearns'.

IV
Saturday Night

Saturday Night

Kesson sent this poem to Peter Calvocoressi at Chatto & Windus in 1960, just for his interest, and read it on the Third Programme some weeks later. There it was called 'Saturday', and featured in a programme called *New Poetry* on 23 April.

'Hang down your head, Tom Dooley' was a hit popular song at the time, sung by Lonnie Donegan, about a young outlaw faced with capital punishment after killing a girl on a mountainside.

V
Radio

Free for All!

This piece celebrates the excitement of childhood, and in particular the approach of Christmas in the Elgin slum. Kesson had published *The White Bird Passes* in 1958, having written and rewritten, ruthlessly pruning the material of the novel to her desired aim, 'the sma' perfect'. She returned to this material more than once, notably in the short story 'Once in Royal . . .' in *Where the Apple Ripens* (1985). 'Free For All!' was written for radio, and read by Kesson in December 1960.

Somewhere Beyond

This is the sequel to the second play that Kesson called 'The Childhood', the autobiographical one which I have called 'The Childhood (2)' (1952). It deals with the years following her life in the orphanage—at the age of fifteen, she was moved from the protection of the orphanage first into a Working Girls' Hostel and then to a Mental Hospital.

It was first broadcast in February 1962 from Glasgow, produced by David Thomson for the Third Programme, starring Lennox Milne as Narrator and Mary Carron, and also featuring Helena Gloag, Gwyneth Guthrie, Effie Morrison, Bryden Murdoch, Jean Taylor Smith, Gudrun Ure and Mary Walton. It is closely based (with omissions) on Kesson's own life after leaving school and orphanage, and being returned there in disgrace, sacked for incompetence and lack of concentration from her first job in a local farm kitchen. She was sent to Aberdeen Academy to do a commercial training, a path just as unlikely to suit her as the farm kitchen. She did not do very well. She lived in St Katherine's Hostel in the Spital, later a YWCA, and was a protégée of the organiser of St Katherine's Club in West North Street, now the Lemon Tree. Miss Bella Walker (Miss Erskine in the play) was a noted pioneer of the welfare of city young people, and the probation service.

As the play makes clear, it was the hostel Matron's snide hostility and references to her mother, a small-time prostitute, that provoked Kesson at last to attack her, and end up spending a year in the mental hospital at Cornhill in Aberdeen. But one crucial element that aided her recovery was the re-encounter with Charge Nurse Fraser who had been a maid at the Skene orphanage when Kesson first went there. Her recognition of the patient and her continuity as a person meant a great deal to the girl.

This is Kesson's most sustained and successful treatment of her breakdown and her hospital experience, but by no means the only one. She had dealt movingly with the same material in 'And That Unrest', a radio play directed by Elizabeth Adair in 1950, and she and Adair collaborated in a treatment for television which was probably never actually offered to the BBC. A short story version, 'Morning Has Broken', was read by Janet Michael on Radio 4 Scotland on 13 July 1977, produced by Stewart Conn. Another short story version, 'Good Friday', is printed in *Where the Apple Ripens*, and was originally published in *Chapman* 27/8. In part this follows 'Morning Has Broken' word for word, but it incorporates a visit from the patient's friend Ginny and her new friend, as in some radio versions.

VI
Moment of Communication

Moment of Communication with a List D girl

From typescript, March 1973. Kesson was working with troubled teenagers in Haddington, East Lothian.

List D: a term for certain categories of what used to be called juvenile delinquents.

VII
Single Journey

Single Journey

Any previous publication so far untraced. Typescript is dated 10 September 1973. At this point, Kesson was living at Smeaton, East Lothian, writing, and working with disturbed teenagers.

Fruit and vegetable traders moved out of Covent Garden in 1974 to a new market at Nine Elms, south of the Thames. However, popular protest forced Greater London Council to abandon its demolition plans. The old market's arcades have been refurbished to become the centrepiece of an area now noted for fashionable shops and restaurants.

VIII
The Useless One

The Useless One: Chronicle of Failure

This has not previously been published, and is taken from a typescript, undated, but probably 1978/9. Kesson was trying to find a form for her (never finally written) autobiography. It was to be entitled *Mistress of None*, and was later changed, quoting Thoreau, to *A Different Drum*, but Kesson found the task of sustained autobiography impossibly difficult for a number of reasons.

The initial quotation is slightly misquoted from John Calder's Introduction to *New Writing And Writers* 15 (1978) where the novella 'Where the Apple Ripens' was first published. A comparison with 'Somewhere Beyond' shows that the one does not mention work in a big store, while the other omits to mention going back to school for the Commercial course. Kesson always seemed intent on obscuring her age at specific times, and how long she spent where, and doing what! The store in question was almost certainly Isaac Benzies, a fashion emporium on George Street, Aberdeen. She was unemployed for a time after being sacked from this second job.

Some of the material in this account can be found in different guises in the radio play 'Friday', unpublished, 1966, in 'Stormy Weather' in *Where the Apple Ripens*, in 'Cold in Coventry', a radio play directed by Marilyn Imrie in December 1991, and in a short story of the same name published in *A Writers Ceilidh for Neil Gunn* edited by Aonghas MacNeacail, also in 1991, and reprinted in this *Companion*.

IX
Later Poems

Elegy

Revisiting Skene with film director Michael Radford in search of locations for his film of *The White Bird Passes* in 1979, Kesson found the tombstone of a younger school fellow in the graveyard.

Evelyn Mary Youngson was a daughter of the farm where Kesson had her first disastrous job as 'kitchie deem'. She was in a lower class than the author at school in Skene.

The poem has also been printed as 'Elegy in Skene Kirkyaird'. First published in *Chapman* 50-51, 1987.

Untitled

('Mama Mia') MS from a draft letter to Avril and Bill Wilbourne, Kesson's daughter and son-in-law, written during preparation for the radio version of *Another Time, Another Place* in 1979/80.

Kesson first intended the words to be spoken by the Italian POW Luigi, but the final version of Luigi could hardly voice such gravitas. Kesson admits in this letter that it is more about her own mother.

Spell Binders

An adult's retrospect of the clamorous Close life in the Elgin of 'Free for All!' or 'Anybody's Alley'. From a typescript dated June 1984. First published with minor changes in *Chapman* 50-51. Elsewhere also entitled 'Loss'.

Somebody

From a typescript dated June 1984. First published with minor changes in *Chapman* 50-51. Kesson wrote progressively fewer poems, and it is very unusual to find Scots in such a late one.

X
Reunion

Reunion

A television play directed by David Blair in December

1991. The single acting role was a triumph for the late Anne Kirsten, who played Jessie superbly, and even contrived to look very like her! From a reading copy dated 1990. This last piece appropriately returns to the autobiographical mode, and even more appropriately attempts to square the circle. See Introduction.

The poetry quoted on p161 is from Poe's 'Annabel Lee', and the final quotation is the whole text of Helen B Cruickshank's poem, 'The Wishin' Well'.

XI
Cold in Coventry

Cold In Coventry

With its overlaps in subject-matter with both 'Reunion' and 'The Useless One', this story vividly illustrates the difficulty of carving out a selection of Kesson's oeuvre, when she worked and reworked so many themes. But it makes a fitting ending for this volume, as it is clear throughout her work and her correspondence that it expresses a great deal of her experience. For the daughter of a prostitute who was reduced to that occupation by the disgrace of pregnancy, and who gave birth in a workhouse, the fear of pregnancy outside marriage was sufficient to ensure that chastity triumphed over inclination. But the insistence that she is not pregnant (true) has to be virtually simultaneous with the suggestion (false) that the returned orphan has had plenty of 'chances'.

This story was first published in *A Writers Ceilidh for Neil Gunn*, edited by Aonghas MacNeacail, 1991.